BOB DYLAN

A LERNER BIOGRAPHY

BOB

Voice of a Generation

DYLAN

Jeremy Roberts

LERNER PUBLICATIONS COMPANY /MINNEAPOLIS

For Robert, with love, angst, and blood on the tracks . . .

Text © 2005 by Jim DeFelice

Lerner Publications Company
A division of Lerner Publishing Group
241 First Avenue North
Minneapolis, MN 55401 U.S.A.

Website address: www.lernerbooks.com

Library of Congress Cataloging-in-Publication Data

Roberts, Jeremy, 1956-
    Bob Dylan : voice of a generation / by Jeremy Roberts.
       p.   cm. — (Lerner biographies)
    Includes bibliographical references and index.
    ISBN: 0–8225–1368–4 (lib. bdg. : alk. paper)
    1. Dylan, Bob, 1941—Juvenile literature. 2. Rock musicians—
United States—Biography—Juvenile literature. I. Title. II. Lerner
biography.
    ML3930.D97R63 2005
    782.42164'092—dc22   2004002460

Manufactured in the United States of America
1 2 3 4 5 6 – JR – 10 09 08 07 06 05

CONTENTS

Teens go wild for rock-and-roll music at a concert in the 1950s. The new sound captured the hearts and minds of young people, including Bobby Zimmerman's.

PRELUDE TO GLORY

The music blared from the radio in the basement of the Zimmerman house in the small town of Hibbing, Minnesota. The young teenager who was listening had never heard anything quite like it. Most of the songs on the local radio station were slow tunes played by large bands and orchestras. That music was more likely to put him to sleep than get him excited. But this music jumped out of the tiny radio like pure energy. It had an electric guitar and a loud drum. The hard beat combined to produce a new sound known as rock and roll.

When the song faded, the boy ran upstairs to the family's upright piano. He pounded the keys, imitating what he had heard. As he played, the young man dreamed of fortune and fame. Although he couldn't read music, he had a knack for recreating what he heard. He also had a gift for using words. As he banged out a tune, words sprang into his head to go with the music.

The young man was Bobby Zimmerman. In just a few years, he'd be known to the world as Bob Dylan. He would first change folk music, and then rock and roll, forever. His songs would voice the dreams of an entire generation. Many would call him a prophet.

But tonight he had to calm the energy the music had inspired. It was a school night in the 1950s and time to get changed for bed and go to sleep. His life as a rock star and musician existed only in his imagination.

Immigrants arrive in the United States at New York City's Ellis Island in the early 1900s. Bobby's grandparents arrived during that time period.

chapter one
ROOTS
and MUSIC

From its very beginning as a nation, the United States has been a land of opportunity and promise. Immigrants arrive hoping to practice religion freely and give their opinions without fear. In the United States, immigrants can forge new identities as Americans.

Bobby Zimmerman's Jewish grandparents arrived as immigrants from eastern Europe during the early years of the 1900s. The call of freedom was strong. Zigman Zimmerman left a good job running a factory in Odessa, Russia, to become a peddler in the United States, selling everyday goods to other immigrants. He came to Duluth, Minnesota, in 1907 and soon sent for his wife and children. Bobby's father, Abraham "Abe" Zimmerman, was born in 1911. Abe found a job as a messenger with Standard Oil when he was sixteen. His hard work helped him keep his job during the Great Depression of the 1930s, when more than one-quarter of the U.S. workforce was unemployed. In 1932 he met a Jewish girl named Beatrice "Beatty" Stone, also known as "Bea" to friends. She also was the daughter of Jewish immigrants. The two young people fell in love and married in 1934. On May 24, 1941, they had their first child, Robert Allen Zimmerman. As observant Jews, they gave him a Hebrew name: Shabtai Zisel ben Avraham. Most of his family and friends knew him as "Bob" or "Bobby."

In 1946, shortly after the birth of the family's second son, David, Abe caught polio, a devastating disease. At the time, there was no cure for polio, which attacked a person's spinal chord. A bad case could kill or cripple someone. Bobby's father survived but limped for the rest of his life. His health was damaged so severely that he could not return to his job at Standard Oil. Instead, he and two of his brothers opened an appliance store in Hibbing, fifty-eight miles northwest of Duluth, where Bea had grown up.

In the 1940s, Duluth was a growing city. Hibbing, however, was starting to decline. The ground around it had once been filled with rich deposits of iron ore. Once the ore was mined and processed, it could be used for iron and steel. These important materials were used to build everything from railways to skyscrapers as the United States grew. But Hibbing's mines were nearly exhausted. Old ore dumps lay scattered around the town, the clumps of rocks overgrown with weeds and trees.

Six-year-old Bobby adjusted to the new neighborhood, making friends and playing in the yards and lots nearby. "Usually he was fun to be with," Larry Furlong, a boyhood friend, said. "He wasn't spoiled. He seemed no different than any of the kids in the neighborhood. But I do remember that his feelings could be hurt easily." Kids sometimes teased Zimmerman by making fun of his unusual last name, calling him "Zennerman" or something similar. As he grew toward his teen years, Bobby seemed to become shy and more sensitive. But he was always a good student, quick and intelligent.

Bobby *(inset)* attended this synagogue (Jewish house of worship) in Hibbing, Minnesota. A good religious student, Bobby also had a love and talent for music.

He easily mastered the Hebrew necessary for bar mitzvah (the entry of a Jewish boy into the adult Jewish community), impressing his teachers with his ability.

Rock and Roll and Other Influences

Like many other young teenagers in the mid-1950s, Bobby was intrigued by the early music of rock-and-roll performers. Early rock and roll developed from rhythm and blues, which itself developed from folk, country, and jazz music. Many musicians combined the different styles, experimenting with new sounds and rhythms.

Early rock and roll used guitars as the main instruments. A bass guitar—a four-stringed instrument that played low notes on the musical scale—usually set the beat along with a drum. Another musician used an amplified six-string guitar to play "lead," the notes that made up the song's tune. Another electric guitar would be used to play the "rhythm" of a song,

usually the chords that gave body to the music. Besides the big bass drum used to set the basic beat, the drummer would play cymbals and a snare drum. In some bands, a piano or organ took the lead part instead of a guitar. A saxophone might add variety to the sound.

But the most important member of a rock-and-roll band as far as most fans were concerned was the singer. The singer "fronted" or led the band and became a real star. Many of the early rock-and-roll singers were considered sexy and a little dangerous—for many reasons. Their songs often spoke of sex at a time when this was considered unusual and even wrong. Some had gotten into trouble with the law for minor crimes. A large number of early rock musicians were black. Because of racial prejudice, many white adults objected to white teenagers listening to music by black performers. For many teens, however, this made the music more attractive. Listening to it was an easy way to rebel against parents and other adults.

Among famous early rock and rollers was Little Richard, who won fame for songs such as "Tutti Frutti," which included references to sex. Chuck Berry, another early rock-and-roll star, was known for his guitar work as well as his singing and songwriting. Elvis Presley, considered by many the first white rock superstar, was known for his wild, hip-shaking movements as well as his singing.

But Bobby didn't listen just to early rock. He also liked country music, especially as played by Hiram "Hank" Williams (1923–1953). Williams wrote 125 songs, and many are considered classics. His songs talk about feelings that everyone shares. Many are sad, as the titles show: "I'm So Lonesome I Could Cry," "A House without Love," and "I Just Don't Like This Kind of Living."

Hiram "Hank" Williams performs in the late 1940s. Williams's country music career—cut short by an early death at the age of 29 in 1953—touched millions, including Bobby Zimmerman. Decades later, Williams's songs remain popular with music fans and musicians.

DYLAN'S FIRST GUITAR

The door to the house opened and Bobby Zimmerman rushed in, carrying a trumpet case under his arm. He'd just rented the instrument from a music store downtown. He was excited by the sound and wanted to play. Bobby practiced loud and often for the next few days. But he and the instrument didn't get along. Finally, with the walls still shaking from his sour wails, he returned it to the music store.

He came back with a saxophone. The result was the same. He just couldn't make it sound like anything he liked. A few days later, the sax went back to the shop. The young man kept experimenting until finally he rented an inexpensive guitar. And this time, he found success.

Sounds like a great story, doesn't it? Bob Dylan told biographer Robert Shelton that was how he started playing guitar, and Shelton included it in his book *No Direction Home—The Life and Music of Bob Dylan*, one of the best biographies written about Dylan. There's only one problem—other biographers, looking at Dylan's early past, say it's not true. Dylan made up the story.

Figuring out what really happened in the past can be a tough job for any biographer or historian. Memories are not always reliable, and often there are many views of the same event. In Dylan's case, separating fact from fiction can be even more difficult. He liked to make up stories about his past. Sometimes he did this to make his past seem more adventurous. Other times, he was just having a little fun. Biographers are on their guard. They try to check everything with different witnesses. Even so, there are many things about Dylan's personal life that they do not know for sure.

Shadow Blasters and More

In fall 1956, Bobby and three friends formed a rock band called the Shadow Blasters. Bobby played piano and was the group's lead singer. Mostly the teenagers played for themselves and a few friends, but they did perform at a Hibbing High School pep rally the following spring. "Legend has it the performance ended with Bobby breaking the piano pedal," writes biographer Clinton Heylin. Whether Dylan really broke the pedal or not, he played with a great deal of enthusiasm, stomping and strutting in true rock-and-roll style.

Adults at the school rally reacted to the show with shock, but Bobby's fellow students loved it. Friends noticed that Bobby came out of his shell when he played music. Offstage in class, he seemed quiet and "nerdy." As a performer, though, he had the look of a star, dancing wildly and greasing his hair like a hero in a teen movie of the time.

The Shadow Blasters soon fell apart. In 1957 Bobby formed a new band called the Golden Chords. The band mostly did "covers"—their version of someone else's songs. But Bobby also wanted to write his own music. "He'd hear a song and make up his own version of it," said Leroy Hoikkala, the Golden Chords' drummer.

The Golden Chords played at school functions and even at a small local club. After two of the band members left to join another group that summer, Bobby started fresh once more. He turned from piano to guitar—an instrument more suited to leading a rock band. He briefly joined a group in Duluth, where his cousin Stevie Goldberg gave him advanced guitar lessons. For the rest of his high school years, he played with several different bands, continuing to improve his abilities and often insisting on doing things his own way. Then, sometime around 1958, Bobby Zimmerman heard something on a record that immediately changed his musical direction.

Odetta

In the 1950s, popular music was sold on records, thin plastic discs with a diameter of seven or twelve inches. Each played at a different speed on a record player. "Singles" had one song on each side of the record and were played at forty-five revolutions per minute (rpms). "Albums," the larger record, held about thirty minutes of sound on each side. These were played at thirty-three and one-third rpms. (Singles were often called "forty-fives" and albums, "records.") Record stores often allowed customers to play songs on a record player before buying them.

One day Bobby went into a store and pulled out an album that had been made two years before. The music affected him like nothing he had heard before. Called *Odetta Sings Ballads and Blues,* the album had been made by a tall, black singer born Odetta Holmes but known to music fans simply as Odetta. The album included folk songs written decades and, in some cases, hundreds of years earlier. Deep and rich, Odetta's voice made the songs of sadness and hope unforgettable.

In the 1950s, Bobby heard a record by Odetta *(below, left).* He instantly connected with the heartfelt lyrics and music of the African American performer's folk and blues.

The term *folk music* refers to old or traditional songs played on guitars or other simple instruments. These songs have often been passed from one generation to another and cover a wide range of topics and styles. The term also refers to new music written in that style.

Most traditional folk songs started as popular music enjoyed by many people in other lands. The music came to America with the first Europeans. Slaves and immigrants from Africa added their sounds to the music as well. Some people also considered religious hymns and gospel music sung in church as folk music. These different origins made for a wide range of songs and styles. "Folk music is the only music where it isn't simple," said Dylan, talking about how hard it was to define the music. "It's...full of legend, myth, Bible and ghosts." The words in most folk songs are meant to be listened to and thought about, even studied like poems.

Around the 1900s, union organizer Joe Hill began using music in his campaigns to help laborers get better working conditions. The connection between folk music and radical politics strengthened as the labor struggles continued. In the 1950s and early 1960s, folk music, especially songs with religious themes, were used in the fight for equal rights for African Americans.

During the late 1950s and 1960s, the United States was in the middle of a folk revival. While the music was not as popular as rock and roll, it enjoyed a much wider audience than it had in previous years. Many coffeehouses and small clubs featured the music. Folk performers had television specials, and record companies released many albums of folk songs. Unlike rock and roll, folk music appealed to older people as well as teenagers and young adults.

Scholars debate the exact dates of the folk revival, but they usually consider it to be from the late 1950s to the mid-1960s. Folk music remains an important style for contemporary musicians.

FOLK MUSIC

"I went out and traded my electric guitar and amplifier for an acoustical guitar, a flat-top Gibson," Bobby said years later. "I learned all the songs on that record." The songs were "vital and personal." He felt their emotion right away. Some made him sad, some happy. All made him want to sing. Bobby began listening to all the folk music he could find, learning to play it on an acoustic guitar.

After Odetta, Bobby listened to other popular folksingers, such as the Kingston Trio, a folk group that started in San Francisco, California, during the 1950s. The Kingston Trio wrote folk songs and performed them with smooth harmonies and catchy rhythms. Bobby then learned about artists such as the Carter Family and Jesse Fuller. These performers were more traditional. Their music sounded rougher and included fiddles (or violins), autoharps (stringed instruments), harmonicas, and even kazoos (small, tubular instruments). These artists played songs that had been handed down for generations.

GUITARS

Though acoustic and electric guitars are played the same way, each has a different sound. An electric guitar's sound is controlled by a volume switch on the amplifier. The sound is best when it's energetic and even brash. Played well, an electric guitar makes people want to jump up and dance.

Electric guitars are great in large halls, where loudspeakers can boom their sound. An acoustic guitar doesn't use an amplifier. Its sound is much softer and more personal. If playing an electric guitar is like shouting in a crowd, playing an acoustic guitar is like whispering in a small living room.

Looking like the "boy next door" in his Hibbing High School class photo, senior Bobby Zimmerman had plans to be anything but common. He had set his sights on rock-and-roll glory.

Bob Dylan

When Bobby Zimmerman graduated from Hibbing High School in 1959, his yearbook entry declared that he was going to "join Little Richard" and become a rock star. He gave a concert that spring at the school that seemed to prove it.

But just in case that idea didn't work out, he planned to attend college, probably because his mom wanted him to. Bob enrolled at the University of Minnesota in Minneapolis as a liberal arts student. He started going to classes that fall. By October he had found an area of the city near campus known as Dinkytown. It was full of coffeehouses and other places where musicians and artists performed and hung out.

Bob began performing folk songs at a small coffeehouse called the Ten O'Clock Scholar. Before long, he was playing there and at parties regularly. He stopped going to classes, spending all his time playing guitar.

"Bob just drifted in," said an old acquaintance, "Spider John" Koerner, who also played folk music there. "He was writing some songs, but they were those folksy spirituals. . . . [He] had a very sweet voice, a pretty voice, much different from what it became."

Bobby Zimmerman was playing folk music, not rock and roll. The music differed greatly from what he had been performing just a few months before in Hibbing. But he had changed something even more important—his name. He'd started calling himself Bob Dylan.

While attending the University of Minnesota, Zimmerman wrote songs and played gigs in the hip Minneapolis college neighborhood of Dinkytown, calling himself Bob Dylan.

There are many different stories about why Robert Zimmerman chose "Dylan" as his last name. The most popular story—and the one most biographers believe is true—is that he chose the name because he liked the poetry of a Welsh poet named Dylan Thomas. Dylan Thomas wrote the story (later made into a popular play) *A Child's Christmas in Wales* and many poems popular at the time. But in later years, Bob Dylan denied this. Instead, he told biographers and journalists that the name came from uncles or members of his mother's family. While many biographers doubt this, the exact origin of the name remains a mystery, one encouraged by Bob Dylan himself.

Wherever the name came from, selecting it was important. It helped the young man reinvent himself as a folksinger. He was no longer Bobby Zimmerman, shy kid from a small town. He was Bob Dylan, folksinger.

Woody

Dylan wasn't very interested in his college classes, but he studied music fiercely. He borrowed albums and taught himself all sorts of new songs and styles. He played and he played and he played. During the summer of 1960, Dylan took a trip to Denver, Colorado. He stayed for several weeks, performing there. When he came back to Minneapolis, friends realized just how much he was learning. Even in the short time that he'd been gone, he had become a much better performer. His guitar playing sounded better. He seemed more comfortable when singing. He joked between songs and made people anxious to hear more.

Dylan also found new folksingers to copy. The most important was Woody Guthrie, one of the greatest songwriters and folksingers in the United States. Guthrie wrote more than one thousand songs, including such famous ones as "This Land Is Your Land," a celebration of the beauty and spirit of the United States. Guthrie also wrote many songs about the Great Depression.

Dylan was inspired by the songwriting and music of folksinger Woody Guthrie *(left)*. Guthrie's social and political brand of folk has influenced musicians across many music genres (classifications) and remains a musical cornerstone.

Woody Guthrie was probably the "singingest" man that ever was. No American songwriter wrote more songs or influenced more musicians and just plain folks than he did. Yet Guthrie was poor most of his life, or he lived as if he were poor.

Born in 1912 in Okemah, Oklahoma, Woodrow W. Guthrie grew up in a booming oil town. His early life was filled with tragedy. His sister Clara died young. His mother was stricken with a disease that disabled her for life. His father lost all his money at the start of the Great Depression (1929– 1942).

Guthrie moved to Texas in 1931, where he worked as a sign painter and musician. He married his first wife, Mary Jennings, the sister of a musician friend. The couple had three children. As the Depression deepened, he left his family and joined the millions of unemployed workers headed to find work in California.

With his guitar on his back, Guthrie walked on dust-choked roads. He rode ramshackle trucks with families who had lost their farms. He hopped empty freight cars and shared scraps of food with other homeless men. Wherever he went, Guthrie sang old folk songs and wrote new ones about the things that were happening around him. Many of Guthrie's songs may not have been written down, but he is known to have written more than three thousand. The topics ranged from love songs to protest songs to songs celebrating the Jewish faith.

Guthrie's music found a wider audience after he reached California in 1937. He was discovered by a local radio personality and had a show on KFVD, a popular Los Angeles station. He also became known for his willingness to play at union protests and political gatherings. He championed fairness for all, especially regular people who had become poor because of the Depression. Guthrie turned his personal experiences into songs with names like "Dust Bowl Blues," "Hard Traveling," and "I Ain't Got No Home." In 1939 he wrote "This Land Is Your Land" while hitchhiking to New York City. The song remains one of the most famous celebrations of the United States ever written.

By 1954 Guthrie's traveling days were over. He had inherited Huntington's chorea, a disease that gradually destroyed his muscles and nervous system. Over the next thirteen years, he slowly lost the ability to walk, to write, and play guitar. He died in 1967. His book, *Bound for Glory*, gives an excellent glimpse of his life and times.

THE MUSIC & POLITICS OF WOODY GUTHRIE

Besides playing guitar, Guthrie accompanied himself on harmonica, using a brace to hold it in place while he played. Dylan started doing the same. He also changed his voice to sing in the rough style Guthrie had used. The sound seemed to come from someone who had worked in the fields as a farmer all his life. This style was considered "authentic," or real, making the singer sound as if he sang from personal experience about a hard job or a sad life.

By the fall of 1960, Bob Dylan was a well-known regular at local parties and coffeehouses in Minneapolis and nearby Saint Paul. But he longed for a bigger stage. He also longed to meet Woody Guthrie, who at the time had

A young woman walks with her guitar in New York City's Greenwich Village neighborhood. Dylan set out for the Village—the thriving center of the U.S. folk music scene—in late 1960.

been hospitalized in New Jersey for Huntington's chorea, a severe inherited disorder of the nervous system. The disease destroys brain cells and causes involuntary body movements, mental disturbances, and eventually death.

In the winter of 1960–1961, Bob Dylan and a friend, Bob Underhill, began hitchhiking to New York City. Guthrie was in a hospital nearby, and Dylan hoped to visit him. Dylan also wanted to visit New York City, which was then home to many folk musicians. The city had many coffeehouses and other places to perform. Almost anyone interested in folk music eventually ended up there, if only to visit. On January 24, 1961, so did Bob Dylan.

Owner Art D'Lugoff stands at the door of his folk and blues club, the Village Gate, in Greenwich Village in the early 1960s. If Dylan was to be successful, he'd have to get regular gigs at popular clubs like this one.

chapter two

GREENWICH VILLAGE

The stairs up from the subway were covered with snow. The winter of 1960–1961 was one of New York's coldest and snowiest. Even Bob Dylan, who was from the Upper Midwest, felt the chill. But despite the frigid weather, the narrow streets around the New York City neighborhood of Greenwich Village were on fire with folk music.

Soon after he hitchhiked to New York, Dylan found a club called Café Wha?. The club hosted open mike nights, when anyone could come up onstage and sing. Dylan played a few songs. When the club owner learned that Dylan and his friend Underhill had almost no money, the owner announced to the audience that the young men needed a place to stay. Someone took them in for the night. For the next few months, Dylan slept—or "crashed"—wherever he could. He often slept on the floors of people he'd barely met.

Dylan didn't see this situation as much of a hardship. He spent most of his time talking to other folk musicians and learning from them. He hung out backstage at a small club playing "Muleskinner Blues," learning new ways to play, and swapping songs. He graduated from playing for free to performing at small clubs where musicians passed around a hat or basket to collect tips. Underhill eventually went home, but Dylan stayed. He didn't have much, but he was determined to keep learning.

"When Bobby came in to work the first time," said Mike Porco, "I didn't know if he had enough clothes." Porco owned a folk club named Gerde's Folk City, where Dylan and many other young singer-songwriters performed. Porco gave him some clothes and helped him join the musicians' union. (The better-known clubs required musicians to be union members if they wanted to perform.) By the end of March, Porco offered Dylan a gig, or music job, appearing for two weeks as the regular act.

A folk musician plays to a packed house at Gerde's Folk City in Greenwich Village. Dylan landed his first gig at the club in March 1961, just a few months after arriving in New York City.

Dylan was called back to Gerde's in April 1961 as the warm-up act (the performer before the main act) for world-renowned blues singer John Lee Hooker. Sharing the bill (show flier and performance lineup) with headliners helps up-and-coming performers get the public exposure they need. The performers are often listed in order of popularity, with stars getting top bill.

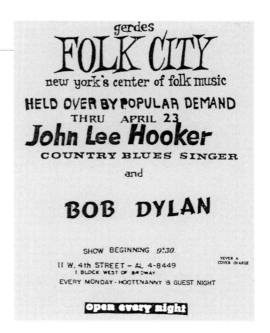

The two-week performance at Gerde's paid a little more than ninety dollars a week, a good sum at the time. Most of Dylan's gigs were for much less. He hustled for work and continued to rely on friends. Romantic relationships often provided him with a place to stay, if only for a night. "He had a lot of nerve with girls. More than I did," said a friend named Mark Spoelstra. "Chasing them, coming on to them, not being intimidated—man, Dylan was remarkable." But no friendship or love relationship was as important as Dylan's friendship with Woody Guthrie.

Greystone Hospital

Greystone Hospital loomed over the New Jersey landscape like a dark, forbidding castle. While its grounds were beautiful, its halls were filled with wails and odd noises. Many of the patients in this state-funded hospital had serious mental illnesses and developmental diseases. Woody Guthrie called it "the prettiest . . . booby hatch I came across."

Dylan walked through the dreary corridors to visit his idol in late January 1961. Guthrie was old and sick, and often in pain. His body sometimes jerked uncontrollably, but Dylan wasn't put off. He sang for his hero. Dylan soon became a regular visitor, not just at the hospital but at the home of Guthrie's friends Sidsel and Bob Gleason. They lived in East Orange, New Jersey, not far from the hospital, and Guthrie often spent weekends at their home. Many folksingers who knew Guthrie would show up as well. Music was a natural part of these informal get-togethers. For Bob Dylan, the weekends were like advanced classes in folk music.

"Bobby sort of hung back in the shadows," remembered Ramblin' Jack Elliott. Elliott was a folksinger and a close friend of Guthrie. Elliott had played all across the United States and in Europe. He was also well known in Great Britain. "Bob was shy then. . . . But right off I could see that Bob was very much influenced by everything about Woody."

Among the first songs that Dylan wrote after arriving in New York was "Song to Woody." The song is a tribute to Guthrie. In it Dylan says he will follow in his hero's footsteps and become a famous folksinger.

Breakthrough

The change in Dylan's musical abilities astounded friends back in Minneapolis when he returned for a brief visit that spring and early summer. "In a mere half year he had learned to chum up [play] exciting, bluesy, hard-driving-harmonica-and-guitar music," said John Pankake, who edited a local folk magazine. When Dylan went back to New York, though, he

THE SIXTIES

When people say the "sixties," they're usually referring to more than just the decade. Writers and historians often use the term as shorthand to refer to a time of immense change in American society and culture. The fight for civil rights and the war in Vietnam (1954–1975), along with advances in technology and booming prosperity, seemed to mark the end of something old and the beginning of something new. Sometimes these changes came with violence. While many protests against the war and for civil rights were peaceful, some became riots and resulted in deaths. President John Kennedy, his brother Senator Robert Kennedy, and civil rights leader Martin Luther King Jr. were all assassinated during the decade.

At the start of the 1960s, many young people were extremely hopeful. They believed that they could change the world for the better. Turned off by the failures of traditional leaders, they sought new models to follow. By the early 1970s, many young people no longer had such high hopes. They were saddened by the ongoing violence of the Vietnam War and in society. They felt that many of their goals, such as equal rights for blacks and women, had not been achieved.

Still, the sixties were a time of great change, much of it—such as the Civil Rights Acts of 1964 and 1968—positive. Looking back, many remember the times for the hopes and aspirations of the young people who lived through them.

struggled to earn money and often went hungry. He tried to get a contract with a company to produce a record album but found little interest.

Dylan later said that he decided to write his own songs because he wanted to sing about the things that were happening around him. Some of these things, such as the fight for racial equality, were important. Some, such as a fight at a picnic, were a little silly. He wanted to sing about people he knew and things that had happened to him. But silly or serious, he wanted to tell stories with his music that would interest other young people.

Dylan didn't feel that the music to his songs was as important as the words. Many other folksingers shared this view. Songwriters often wrote new words and set them to the tune of an old song. "I don't care about the melodies, man, the melodies are all traditional anyway," Dylan told an interviewer. Dylan tended to write in bursts "at people's houses, people's apartments, wherever I was."

The warm summer brought Dylan—along with crowds of performers and fans—to Washington Square, a park at the edge of Greenwich Village. Dylan remembered, "There could be fifteen jug bands, five bluegrass bands and an old crummy string band, twenty Irish confederate groups, a southern mountain band, folksingers of all kinds and colors." Jug bands were folk groups using homemade instruments. Bluegrass is a type of traditional folk music using the fiddle and other stringed instruments. Dylan used the words *Irish confederate* to mean traditional Irish folk music, especially songs calling for the end of British occupation of Northern Ireland.

In late September 1961, Dylan got another gig at Gerde's Folk City. Among those in the audience was Robert "Robbie" Shelton, a music critic at the *New York Times*. The *Times* is one of the most important newspapers in the city and the nation. Shelton had met Dylan the previous summer and liked him, but he hadn't had a chance to write about him. Shelton interviewed Dylan to get some background for his story. What was his name, the reporter asked—Bob or Bobby? People called him both.

"Bob Dylan, Bobby Dylan, Bob Dylan, Bobby Dylan," answered the folksinger. He couldn't decide. Finally, he blurted, "Make it Bob Dylan!"

In November 1961, Dylan received top bill, performing his first concert as a headliner in the Chapter Hall of New York City's prestigious Carnegie Hall. Dylan had become a real presence in New York's folk music scene.

THE FOLKLORE CENTER

Presents

BOB DYLAN

IN HIS FIRST NEW YORK CONCERT

SAT. NOV. 4, 1961   **8:40pm**

CARNEGIE CHAPTER HALL

154 WEST 57th STREET • NEW YORK CITY

All seats $2.00

Tickets available at: The Folklore Center
                         110 MacDougal Street
GR 7 - 5987   New York City 12, New York

Shelton did. In his review, published September 29, 1961, he said, "Although only twenty years old, Bob Dylan is one of the most distinctive stylists to play in a Manhattan cabaret [a musical club] in years."

Shelton wrote that Dylan's voice was "anything but pretty. He is consciously trying to recapture the rude beauty of a Southern field hand musing in melody on his back porch." He described Dylan as a "cross between a choir boy and a beatnik." (The term *beatnik* primarily refers to certain American artists and writers of the 1950s and 1960s who shared a set of literary, political, and social values. The beat movement was characterized by personal alienation and contempt for the conventional. It encouraged stylistic freedom and spontaneity.)

Shelton also noted that Dylan combined humor and tragedy in his songs. He could take a serious subject and make it humorous. For example, his song "Talking Bear Mountain Massacre Blues" turned a riot over tickets to a picnic into a humorous event, showing how pointless fighting can be. But Dylan could also sing about the sad death of a poor homeless man and make people realize they should do more to help their fellow human beings.

After Shelton's article was published, many more people came to hear Dylan. The article may also have helped convince John Hammond Sr., a producer at Columbia Records, to sign Dylan to a five-year contract. Hammond was an important figure in the music world. He had first made his mark as a jazz producer, working with many stars. Among them were Billie Holiday (1915–1959), a well-known jazz singer in the 1930s and 1940s; Benny Goodman (1909–1986), a famous bandleader who was one of the first whites to form a band with both white and black musicians; and Count Basie (1904–1984), a famous bandleader and composer during the 1930s and 1940s.

In November 1961, Hammond brought Dylan to a Columbia studio on Seventh Avenue in New York and began recording. Hammond convinced the president of the record company to listen in. Both were impressed. But the folksinger was more interested in an old black janitor who stopped working to listen. Dylan knew then that his music was good.

When he left the studio, Dylan walked up Seventh Avenue past a record store. "It was one of the most thrilling moments in my life. I couldn't believe that I was staring at all the records in the window, Frankie Laine, Frank Sinatra, Patti Page, Mitch Miller, Tony Bennett and so on and [I realized that] . . . I, myself, would be among them in the window."

Dylan performs a song during a recording session at Columbia Records in 1961. A record release had the potential to bring him national fame.

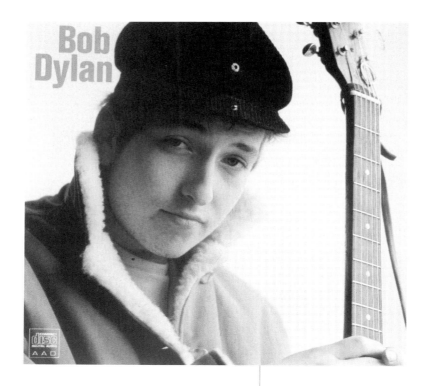

The album, called *Bob Dylan,* came out in March 1962. Most of the songs on it, such as "House of the Rising Sun," a traditional folk song, were written by people other than Dylan. An important exception was "Talking New York," a song that summarizes Dylan's early days in the city.

Dylan's first album, *Bob Dylan,* hit record stores in March 1962. A collection of mainly covers (remakes), on which Dylan struggled to find his voice, the album did not sell well. Columbia nearly canceled Dylan's contract.

Shelton wrote the liner notes, a short biography of the singer included with the album. Because the *New York Times* frowned on reporters doing this, he used the pen name, or alias, of Stacey Williams. But Shelton's use of a different name was hardly the only thing about the liner notes that was invented. Dylan made up much of his supposed background. He told the writer he had lived in Sioux Falls, South Dakota, and Gallup, New Mexico. Fact mixed freely with fiction as Dylan once more reinvented himself.

One thing that Dylan did not make up was his ability to write a song very quickly. He told Shelton that "either the song comes fast, or it won't come at all." And they were coming fast and furiously.

Love

When he wasn't writing or performing folk songs, Dylan was falling in love with a seventeen-year-old high school girl named Suze (pronounced "Suzy") Rotolo. Suze was studying to be a painter. A slim, dark-haired beauty, she was the younger sister of Carla Rotolo, who worked for folk song collector and expert Alan Lomax. Lomax was influential in the folk world and helped promote Dylan's career.

The romance quickly took off. But Suze's mother, Mary Rotolo, disapproved. She thought Suze was too young to have a serious romantic relationship or to get married. And she thought Dylan was a "scruffy beatnik."

Suze may have had her own doubts. She told a friend she didn't want to marry Dylan because she had to "grow up first." But Dylan convinced her to move in with him. They lived together during the winter of 1961–1962, sharing a tiny two-room apartment at 161 West Fourth Street in Greenwich Village. When Suze left to study art in Italy during spring 1962, the separation hurt Dylan deeply. He cried openly and told friends how much he missed her.

Moving On

Although he was heartsick, Dylan continued to write and perform new songs. While critics generally liked his first album, it did not sell very well. At the time, popular folksingers and groups sang their songs with polished voices that sounded smooth and clean. The most popular folksingers were small groups such as the Kingston Trio. The three members of the group blended their voices in harmony and made their songs sound almost as smooth as a large orchestra might sound. In contrast, Dylan's voice sounded rough, even jarring. Although it was much closer to authentic folksinging, the style was not popular.

Dylan recorded new material in the studio and performed before growing audiences in 1962. He also appeared as a guest musician on albums such as this one.

For Dylan, the biggest problem with the album was that he had written only one its songs. The album seemed old to him by the time it was released. Its traditional songs were about the past. His new songs were

about what was going on at the time. He was much more excited about his new work. And so were his audiences, which continued to grow.

In the summer of 1962, Albert Grossman became Dylan's manager. Grossman had represented other folk performers and had many contacts in the music industry. He got Dylan new jobs and negotiated bigger record contracts. But Grossman's help came at a high price. Because of various business arrangements, he took 35 percent of the money earned by Dylan's songs. Dylan himself received only 40 percent. The rest went to the record company that produced the songs. Though the deal was not a good one, it was not unusual at the time for managers to take much of what a new performer earned.

Despite his new manager, times were still hard for Dylan as 1962 continued. He was eager to work on a new album but had to wait until the record company was ready. Ideas were flowing, but his girlfriend was far away, and success seemed even further away. Still, he kept on playing, singing, and writing songs.

Having found his voice, Dylan sang a new song that captivated his audience during a return gig at Gerde's in 1962. "Blowin' in the Wind" would quickly become an anthem for a generation.

chapter three
A CHANGING

The crowd at Gerde's applauded enthusiastically as the young singer finished his song. Barely twenty-one, with a boyish smile and curly hair poking around his ears, the thin young man seemed like the kid down the street. But Bob Dylan's voice had the weathered strain of a world-weary old man.

Dylan leaned toward the microphone. He often introduced his work with rambling stories, most of which had no clear point. But the introduction to his next song wasn't a story at all. He apologized for the tune he had just written and was about to sing. "This here ain't a protest song or anything like that, 'cause I don't write protest songs," he said. "I'm just writing it as something to be said, for somebody, by somebody."

He called the song "Blowin' in the Wind." The words were extremely simple. They asked how long it would be before people lived in peace and harmony. Contrary to what Dylan claimed, it was a protest song. And within a few weeks, "Blowin' in the Wind" became one of the most famous and popular protest songs in the United States. In simple language, it summarized two of the most important conflicts of the early 1960s: the fight for equal rights for blacks and the movement to end the war in Vietnam.

Many young people were deeply concerned about these issues in the early 1960s. Blacks had fought for many years for rights such as the ability to vote and have fair trials. By 1962 leaders such as the Reverend Martin Luther King Jr. had won public attention and were gaining support. Many people who protested against war believed that nuclear weapons threatened all people, not just soldiers. Many worried that the earth would soon be destroyed unless nuclear weapons were banned.

Dylan did not say how these problems should be solved. Instead, his song simply asked how long it would take before someone found solutions. At the same time, the song seemed to urge people to pay attention to the problems and work together to solve them.

PROTEST SONGS

"Blowin' in the Wind" belongs to a special group of songs that experts call protest songs. These songs protest, or criticize, conditions in society. Songs that protest such things as slavery, discrimination, and war have a long history in the United States.

During the twentieth century, music was often used to tell people about difficult working conditions and to encourage unions to stand up for workers' rights. In the 1920s and 1930s, Woody Guthrie and many other folk artists not only wrote songs about union struggles but sang them at gatherings to help encourage workers trying to win fair pay and better working conditions. Dylan, like other folksingers, expanded on this tradition when he began writing and performing songs.

Dylan based the simple tune for his song on a folk song called "No More Auction Block." The song had been sung by freed slaves who had escaped from the Southern slave states to Canada in the early nineteenth century. While there are clear similarities, Dylan re-arranged the tune to fit his song.

Freedom Riders look on as their bus burns following a firebombing. The riders—white and black—rode buses through the South to protest segregation laws in the early 1960s. The riders often met with violent opposition.

Dylan apparently did not think it was a very good song and soon dropped it from his act. But when Peter, Paul, and Mary, a popular folk group, sang it, the song became a hit and helped make Dylan famous.

Hard Rain

In the fall of 1962, folksingers crowded into the back room of one of New York City's most famous and elegant concert halls, Carnegie Hall. Pete Seeger had invited them to perform at a "hootenanny" or folk music festival. Many performers hoping to win new listeners showed up. Too many, in fact.

President John F. Kennedy *(center)* finishes an inspection during the nuclear standoff between the United States and the Soviet Union in the early 1960s. Dylan's "Hard Rain" spoke to a generation faced with civil rights injustices and the threat of nuclear war.

"Folks, you're going to be limited to three songs. No more," said Seeger apologetically. "'Cause we each have ten minutes apiece and no more."

Dylan raised his hand from the thick of the crowd. "What am I supposed to do?" he asked. "One of my songs is ten minutes long."

Anyone else might have told Dylan to choose something else. But Seeger had a hungry curiosity when it came to music, so he listened to the song—and loved it. He gave Dylan his own slot so the young singer would have a block of time long enough to sing his song.

Dylan's song, "A Hard Rain's a-Gonna Fall" ("Hard Rain") was about changes that would take place in society. The song compared justice to a violent storm that would punish those who were evil. But many people who heard the song thought it was about a nuclear disaster. They believed that the song spoke of the need to change the world before it was too late.

The song, which actually runs about seven minutes, is presented as a conversation between a parent and child. The child is like a prophet who has wandered the world and seen all of its injustices. He realizes that God's judgment—the hard rain—is going to come. The parent in "Hard Rain" doesn't play much of a role in the story of the song, though it doesn't take too much imagination to suppose that he or she may have helped cause the problems the young man sees. Dylan builds the song by giving many examples. Some are almost like riddles. Rather than saying directly that blacks face discrimination, for example, he compares them to dogs being walked by whites. The song ends hopefully, as the prophet-son says that he's going back to do the job he knows he must.

PETE SEEGER

Pete Seeger was one of the most important performers in American folk music during the second half of the twentieth century. Seeger wrote and performed many songs regarded as classics. Among his best-known songs are "Turn, Turn, Turn," which uses words from the Bible to celebrate the different seasons and stages of life. Another well-known song is "Where Have All the Flowers Gone," an antiwar song that uses the simple question of the title to talk about the high cost of war.

Besides performing around the nation and encouraging numerous folksingers, Seeger spread traditional music to an entire generation of school children throughout his career. Well before he became famous, Seeger earned his living by playing traditional songs at school assemblies and making classroom appearances. He never stopped doing shows for kids and brought his music to millions. He also helped hundreds of young performers. Seeger formed a folk group called the Weavers with several friends. The group recorded a popular album and played at many concerts together.

For many people in the 1960s, Bob Dylan was not just a great songwriter and performer. Because he sang and wrote about improving society, some young people saw him as a prophet of change.

The word *prophet* comes from Greek words that mean "to speak for." To the ancient Greeks, prophets spoke for the gods. In the history of the Jewish, Christian, and Islamic religions, prophets often said things that people did not want to hear. They spoke of justice, fairness, and God's will. Usually, they were ignored or punished at first, only to be proved correct later.

RELUCTANT PROPHET

Many fans thought of Dylan as a prophet. His songs predicted change. The songs urged justice, fairness, and respect for all people. During the 1960s, Dylan did not preach religion or say that he was a prophet. He did not claim to be a leader. But his powerful songwriting inspired many to fight for equal rights and justice for all. The songs were sung by many who opposed war and wanted all people to live in peace. Because of this, Dylan's songs were considered much more than just music. Popular songs or popular songwriters have had such influence only a few times in history.

In "Hard Rain," Dylan used the simple traditions of folk music to speak about life around him. He repeated phrases several times to make a pleasing pattern of repetition. He used colorful images and poetic language. While his tone was harsher than in "Blowin' in the Wind," once again he captured the feelings and fears of others his age.

Freewheelin'

"Hard Rain" was one of thirteen songs included on Dylan's second album, *The Freewheelin' Bob Dylan,* released in July 1963. Besides "Blowin' in the Wind" and "Hard Rain," four other protest songs were on the album. Because these songs were so good, many people thought Dylan was a protest singer. But he was far too good a songwriter to be described so simply. Most of the other songs were confessional. The singer "confessed" his feelings about things that had happened to him. "Bob Dylan's Dream" did this directly, talking about his early experiences with his friends. In other songs, Dylan took episodes from his life and changed them into stories that could be presented in song. "Girl from the North Country," for example, is written from the point of view of a young man who remembers a girl whom he loved in the north country of Minnesota.

Singing about things he had personally experienced was a far jump from doing classic folk songs written many years before, as he had on his first album. In all his songs, Dylan communicated raw emotion by describing exact detail in simple, direct language. Dylan's listeners shared his emotions and concerns. That helped make the songs important to those who heard them.

Dylan's second album, *The Freewheelin' Bob Dylan,* contained the popular protest songs, "Blowin' in the Wind" and "Hard Rain." The album sold well, but Dylan claimed (and still claims) he was not a protest singer.

Although the songs were inspired by actual events or feelings, Dylan did not intend them to be viewed as a factual life story. On the contrary, he was using what he saw and felt as raw material, but he changed events in the story to make the song better. Poets and fiction writers sometimes say they lie about events to tell the truth about feelings, and this was certainly true for Dylan. He was trying to tell his listeners about emotions and feelings, not about actual events in his life.

Besides writing songs, Dylan was writing poetry and thinking about writing a book. He also drew pictures and sketched. But his talent seemed much better suited to music and songwriting. Songs had to be short and fit into patterns. Others might have found these restrictions confining, but they somehow inspired Dylan.

As Dylan's fame grew, his life became more chaotic. Like many others in the 1960s, he experimented with different drugs, including alcohol and marijuana. Suze returned to the United States, but their relationship began to slide. Dylan began an affair with folksinger Joan Baez, who sang with him at a number of concerts. Suze soon moved in with her sister Carla, but Dylan refused to give her up. Their relationship see-sawed between high points of love and low points of vicious arguments. Much of the emotion found its way into his music.

The Times They Are A-Changin'

Dylan's third album, *The Times They Are A-Changin'*, took its title from one of the songs on the album. Again, the album mixed protest songs with personal songs. Once more, the protest songs drew the most attention.

In "The Times They Are A-Changin'," Dylan speaks to the people of his parents' generation, telling them to either help change the world or to get out of the way so the younger

generation can do it. Written during the summer of 1963, the song joined the idea of protest with another idea becoming popular at the time—the generation gap. While parents and children have always had disagreements in the 1960s, these differences seemed extreme. Many young people thought

Dylan took time off from recording to play the Newport (Rhode Island) Folk Festival in July 1963. He performed with other folk notables, including Peter, Paul, and Mary *(far left),* and Joan Baez *(center).*

their parents were out of touch with the many changes that had taken place in society. The changes ranged from new hair and clothing styles to cable television. Women and blacks were taking jobs they had once been denied. Older people seemed uncomfortable with many of these changes.

The message of the song is that society is bad, but it will soon change. The song echoes some of the ideas in Jesus' Sermon on the Mount in the Bible's New Testament. It includes the line, "Blessed are the meek: for they shall inherit the earth." In Dylan's song, the singer predicts that the poor and forgotten will become society's chosen people. Everything will change. The last will be first. The rich will be poor. By making the speaker a young person, Dylan made the message seem not only urgent but even inevitable.

"Tune in, turn on, drop out." Those words, spoken by Dr. Timothy Leary in 1966, summarized the counterculture movement of the 1960s. The term *counterculture* meant different things to different people, but the term is usually used to describe hippies and others who rejected mainstream society and all that went with it. They dressed in colorful clothing, wore long hair and beads, often used drugs, and did not have regular jobs. A few lived in communes, where they shared property as well as duties. To use Leary's terms, they had "tuned in" to music and the counterculture, "turned on" to drugs, and "dropped out" of society's "rat race," the constant pursuit of money.

THE COUNTERCULTURE
OF THE 1960s

The counterculture was a reaction to the great changes that were happening in society. Many believed that the social wrongs, such as poverty, discrimination, and war, could only be solved by completely rejecting conventional social standards.

The counterculture encouraged people to live without possessions or material wealth. Hippies and others in the counterculture valued creativity, peace, and free love. According to some, all men and women were brothers and sisters who should live in harmony with each other. The government and society's other institutions were often seen as the enemy—or simply irrelevant.

During the late 1950s and early 1960s, some people believed LSD (lysergic acid diethylamide), could make people more creative. Its effects were considered mind-expanding. While the potentially life-threatening dangers of the drug were well known, most ignored them—at least for a short time.

Becoming a hippie was not like joining a club or attending a school. People simply decided to dress and live differently. When they got tired of it, they cut their hair, changed their clothes, and rejoined society.

Civil rights leader Martin Luther King Jr. *(fourth from left)* joins other activists during the 1963 March on Washington. More than 250,000 people marched on Washington, D.C., to demand equal rights and justice.

Like most of Dylan's protest songs, "The Times They Are A-Changin'" has a strong sense of justice behind it. Besides the Sermon on the Mount, it echoes the biblical story of Noah's flood, when, according to the story in the Old Testament, God destroyed the world by making it rain for forty days and nights. Only the creatures on Noah's ark (boat) survived.

The ideal of justice—and the need for it—inspired many people during the 1960s. Martin Luther King Jr. led a massive march on Washington, D.C., in August 1963 to press for racial justice. "I have a dream!" thundered King as he pressed the crowd to work for racial equality. He hoped for a future when whites and blacks could live together in harmony. King wanted everyone to have equal rights and opportunities in life.

"Only a Pawn in Their Game,"
recorded in August 1963 and
sung by Dylan during the
March on Washington, was
released on *The Times They
Are A-Changin'* in January
1964. The album was a clear
return to traditional folk
music, and it sold well with
folk fans.

Dylan attended King's March on Washington and enter-
tained the crowd. He sang "Only a Pawn in Their Game,"
another song from *The Times They Are A-Changin'*. The song
was inspired by the murder of Medgar Evers, a civil rights
worker who was killed earlier in 1963. In the song, Dylan suggested that everyone has responsibility to work for equality.

Songs were often included at civil rights gatherings. Usually, though, the music was older gospel music or old folk
standards, such as "The Battle Hymn of the Republic," which
begins with the words, "Mine eyes have seen the glory of the
coming of the Lord." Dylan's presence at the historic gather-
ing showed not only how famous he had become, but how
important his songs were. His music inspired many to fight
for freedom and equality.

Problems of Fame

With Dylan's records climbing the pop charts, many
reporters from newspapers, magazines, and radio and television stations wanted to do stories on him. Dylan managed to

avoid telling the real story of how he had grown up, which was actually pretty boring. Instead, he hinted that he had had a rough past, sometimes saying he was an orphan, sometimes saying he was a runaway. He implied he had been very poor and on his own.

Dylan invented stories about his past for many reasons. He was naturally a private person and may have felt uncomfortable talking about his family. He also wanted to fit the image of a "real" folksinger that he and others had. Woody Guthrie, for example, had traveled around the country, hopping trains and living a poor man's life. Many early singers of folk and blues had spent much, if not

Dylan performed many shows in the early 1960s to earn fans, earn a living and, some believe, to imitate the lifestyle of folksingers whom he admired.

CORE presents
Bob Dylan
AT UNIVERSITY REGENT THEATRE
680 E. GENESEE STREET
SUNDAY NOV. 3rd AT 4:00 P.M.
Tickets: University Regent Theatre Box office; Corner Store Box Office and for information or reservations call 476-0770 or write Core, 609 E. Adams St., Syracuse, N. Y.

Many of Dylan's young fans liked the edgy, rebel personality popularized by actors such as Marlon Brando *(left)* and James Dean in the late 1950s and early 1960s. They also wanted to see this kind of personality in musicians, and they found it in Dylan's protest songs.

all, of their lives poor and on the road. Many middle-class fans expected folksingers to live such hard lives. Also, during the 1950s, images of troubled youths had been made popular by movies, such as James Dean's *Rebel without a Cause* and Marlon Brando's *The Wild One.* Those images were set in young people's minds. They wanted to rebel from the routine boredom of being middle class, and one way to rebel was to pretend you were not part of it.

Dylan's art depended on invention and reinvention. His songs might have been inspired by an old melody, but then Dylan took over the tune and made it his own. He changed it to make it what he wanted. He did the same thing with his life story. When he wrote his songs, he often invented a character to sing them. This was an old folk tradition. The singer simply pretended that he or she was the person in the story.

For Dylan, imagining himself as a folksinger with a rough past may have helped him become a passionate singer and write passionate, moving songs.

But reporters who accepted his stories as true were upset to find out they were made up. In reaction, those reporters wrote stories that made Dylan look like a liar or a phony. Journalist Andrea Svedburg pointed out some of Dylan's contradictions in a 1963 *Newsweek* article. She wrote about his real past, showing that it was different from the tales he liked to spin. She also pointed out that, while he might say he didn't care about money, he certainly was careful about the business side of his music. "He says he hates the commercial side of folk music, but he has [business managers] who hover about him," wrote Svedburg. Her story also implied that he had taken the words for "Blowin' in the Wind" from someone else. This was completely false, and Dylan got very angry. From that point on, he seldom cooperated with the media.

The charges that he had stolen the words for a song from someone else were part of the darker side of fame. Some people who had known Dylan when he started his career became jealous of his fame as well as his talent. Dylan's personality also encouraged bitter feelings. He could be nasty, especially when he was tired, and his constant schedule of appearances often made him tired. Before he was famous, people were willing to ignore this side of him, either because of the more generous side of his personality or because they realized he had great talent. When he became famous, though, he was considered fair game for attacks by many who didn't even know him. And Dylan was very sensitive to criticism. He even complained onstage at Carnegie Hall about a review J. R. Goddard, a onetime friend, had written.

Gradually, he learned that he had to develop a tough skin to survive media criticism.

Another Side

The year 1964 passed in a blur for Dylan. His relationship with Suze had finally come to an end. His fourth album, titled *Another Side of Bob Dylan,* contained only one protest song. Many of the songs were personal, dealing with the loss of love and the end of love affairs. These heart-wrenching ballads were not really "another side" of Dylan but a side the public had not focused on.

The album did well, but it did not reach the top of the pop charts. Many fans and reviewers criticized Dylan. Irwin Silber, the editor of *Sing Out!* folk magazine, wrote an open letter to Dylan complaining that "your new songs seem to be all inner-directed, . . . inner-probing, self-conscious—maybe even a little maudlin [overly sentimental] or even a little cruel on occasion."

People seemed to be saying that protest songs were all he should do. Protest songs had made Dylan famous, but

Dylan refused to be pigeonholed (classified) by fans and the music industry. In August 1964, he released *Another Side of Bob Dylan.* The album, with its highly personal songs and containing only one protest song, was a departure from his earlier work—work that fans and critics had come to expect. Some were greatly disappointed with the album.

he rebelled. He didn't consider himself a spokesman for political views. For example, people opposed to war and nuclear proliferation (buildup) wanted him to write songs protesting them, but Dylan did not do so. As Shelton put it, he wasn't anyone's "puppet."

Those close to him recognized that he was about to take a huge creative leap. But the public and most Dylan fans had no idea where that leap would go.

At the 1965 Newport Folk Festival, Dylan, with a new look, would also trade his acoustic sound for rock and roll

chapter four
ELECTRIC MUSIC

Night was coming on. All day long, people at the annual folk and blues festival in Newport, Rhode Island, had been buzzing about Bob Dylan. He was supposed to be appearing that night, and rumors about what he would play spread through the crowd.

Finally, musicians came onstage. Many in the audience became restless when they realized it was the Paul Butterfield Blues Band, not Dylan. The group played with electric instruments, and their music was much closer to rock and roll than folk. Why were they at a festival for traditional music?

Suddenly, a man dressed entirely in black walked onstage. He had an electric guitar, which he played loudly. The band ripped into a barely rehearsed version of "Maggie's Farm," a protest song about sharecropping in the South. The song was included on *Bringing It All Back Home,* an album Dylan had released in March 1965.

The man in black was Bob Dylan. Many people recognized him—but not his music. As Dylan shouted into the microphone, the audience was shocked and didn't know how to react.

Dylan played three songs during his electric set *(above)* at the Newport music festival on July 25, 1965. While he disappointed many fans, he changed music that day. Bob Dylan and folk had gone electric.

Some applauded. Many booed. All came away from the Newport festival knowing that the world of music had been changed that night, July 25, 1965. Bob Dylan had become a rock and roller. He had joined the poetry of folk music to the high energy of rock and roll.

Going Electric

No one event had led Dylan to pick up the electric guitar and play folk songs to a rock beat in 1965. Artistically, he wanted to expand what he wrote and played. Dylan wanted to do different songs with different sounds. He wanted to explore.

At about the same time Dylan became popular, the British rock-and-roll band the Beatles took the United States by storm. Playing electric guitars, they appeared on the nationally televised *Ed Sullivan Show* in the fall of 1964. Their massive record sales spurred their style of rock and roll.

Dylan liked the Beatles and their music. He met the group in New York and found that they admired his music. The young musicians quickly became friends and influenced each other. The Beatles began writing songs with poetic images and stories, just as Dylan did. And he started putting his words to the rhythms of rock and roll.

Dylan was not the only performer to combine folk and rock styles. For example, a group called the Animals had a hit with "House of the Rising Sun," a folk ballad included on Dylan's first album. In the spring of 1965, a rock band named the Byrds released a rock-and-roll version of Dylan's song, "Mr. Tambourine Man." It shot up the charts, hitting number one on June 5. Dylan especially liked the Byrds's sound. "They're cutting across all kinds of barriers," he said. "If they don't close their minds, they'll come up with something pretty fantastic."

Dylan *(center)*, with Brian Jones of the Rolling Stones *(left)*, attends a Young Rascals' record release party in 1965. Dylan was fast becoming a shaker and mover on the rock scene.

But no one as famous as Dylan had completely blended the different traditions and styles in new songs. Dylan took the best of both the serious attitude of folk and the energetic beat of rock and made something unique. To fans, the change seemed to happen in an instant, but it was actually a gradual process. Dylan had recorded some songs using electrical instruments with a rocklike beat for his second album, but he left them off the album because he had too much material. On *Bringing It All Back Home,* he used electric instruments and had a sound leaning toward rock and roll. The album *Highway 61 Revisited,* released that August, went much further toward achieving the new rock-and-roll sound.

While most musicians realized the genius of Dylan's new direction, many of his fans were confused and outraged. Even many folksingers were angry, accusing Dylan of selling out. "It was disturbing to the Old Guard," said Jim Rooney, a Boston musician, referring to older folk musicians. "They seemed to understand that night for the first time what Dylan [was] . . . trying to say for over a year—that he is not theirs or anyone else's and they didn't like what they heard and booed."

Some of the boos at the Newport concert may actually have been because of the poor sound system and the short set Dylan played. But after that concert and news stories about it, people booed Dylan wherever he played his new style. Even at the Royal Albert Hall in London, England, nearly a year later, Dylan was heckled.

The Band

Dylan's Newport show with the Paul Butterfield Blues Band was a onetime thing. If he wanted to play rock and roll, he needed to find a regular group of musicians to play with. Sometime during 1965, Dylan heard of the Hawks. The band

Dylan fingers an electric bass while in the recording studio in the mid-1960s. His new brand of electric folk and rock was released on the albums *Bringing It All Back Home* and *Highway 61 Revisited.*

members were Canadians who had toured and played in small clubs for years, performing rhythm and blues songs with a country twang. The sound might be described as something between country and rock and roll with a bit of bluegrass thrown in.

Robbie Robertson, the Hawks' lead guitarist, and drummer Levon Helm joined Dylan for a concert at Forest Hills Stadium in Queens, New York. Eventually, the rest of the group—Rick Danko, Richard Manuel, and Garth Hudson—joined them, and the Hawks became Dylan's official band. Searching for a new name, they soon gave up looking for something fancy and called themselves simply, "the Band." The group played with Dylan for the next several years. They also released albums on their own and became stars in their own right.

Going Home

Dylan saw rock as a return to his roots, as the titles of the two 1965 albums make clear. *Highway 61 Revisited* refers to a U.S. highway that used to run from the Canadian border through the state of Minnesota and south to New Orleans, Louisiana. Dylan saw his musical roots running the same way. (The early rock and roll and blues he had listened to as a boy came from the South.) Among the album's best songs was "Desolation Row." The lyrics painted a complicated, fairy-tale-like story. Characters such as Cinderella and Romeo walked through a modern city where a circus shared space with a beauty parlor. Among the many influences for the song, two appear more important than others. One was the poetry of American beat poet Allen Ginsberg, a friend of Dylan's. Beat poets wanted to break away from everyday society. They did not like traditional styles of art and wanted to invent their own.

Dylan holds lyric cue cards for his song "Subterranean Homesick Blues" in this scene from the documentary *Don't Look Back*. (Poet and friend Allen Ginsberg appears at left.) The documentary was released in 1965, and the popular protest song was released on *Bringing It All Back Home* that same year.

The song also seems to capture the drug experiences of the 1960s. At the time, artists, scientists, and others were experimenting with LSD, a powerful mind-altering drug that makes people hallucinate, or see things that aren't there. The drug was legal in the United States until 1966, and many artists and musicians tried it. (Biographers are not sure whether Dylan actually took the drug. His own statements are unclear.)

Dylan's wild language in that song and many others led reporters to ask what his words meant. But he balked and didn't explain. A listener was supposed to enjoy what he or she could. "Songs are just pictures of what I'm seeing, glimpses of things—life, maybe, as it's going around," said Dylan. "If you don't get it, you don't have to really think about it because it's not addressed to you!"

The album also included "Ballad of a Thin Man." The subject of the song is a journalist who just can't figure out what Dylan is all about. The song became one of his favorites, played over and over at concerts, especially when he thought critics weren't accepting or understanding his new music.

Dylan's *Highway 61 Revisited* reached record stores in late summer 1965. The album contained the hit single, "Like a Rolling Stone," which climbed to number two on several pop charts, bumping songs by the Beatles and the Rolling Stones. Dylan's album became one of the top ten best-sellers that year.

As other musicians took Dylan's lead and combined folk with rock, writers began labeling the new sound "folk-rock." Dylan himself didn't like the term. "It don't matter what kind of nasty names people invent for the music," he said. "It could be called arsenic music." His only real interest was writing the music and singing it. As far as he was concerned, labels didn't matter.

Marriage

Dylan's career rocketed ahead. He was writing and recording music at a furious pace. At the same time, he sought peace and quiet with Sara Lowndes, a former model. Dylan met Sara while vacationing in Woodstock, New York, a small rural village popular with artists. Sara became his lover and inspired his writing. He wrote many songs about her and about their love for each other, including "Sad Eyed Lady of the Lowlands" (1966) and "Sara" (1975). They married in November 1965, after she became pregnant. Dylan adopted her daughter Maria. Together, the couple had four more children, Jesse, Anna, Samuel, and Jakob.

Dylan tried hard to shelter Sara and the children from the media to protect their privacy. Dylan taught the children to stay away from photographers. Both parents worked hard to keep the children from the crazier aspects of his fame. They mostly succeeded. In fact, even biographers at times have had to guess about the number of children they had.

Motorcycle Blues

As the spring of 1966 came to an end, Dylan's popularity peaked. A new album called *Blonde on Blonde* was scheduled for release that summer, with a long tour planned to promote it. A TV program would be aired in the fall, and *Tarantula,* a

BOB DYLAN
Blonde on Blonde

Released May 16, 1966, Dylan's *Blonde on Blonde* was a two-record set—a first in rock and pop genres. Including the songs "Rainy Day Women," "Visions of Johanna," and "Stuck Inside of Mobile," the album appealed to folk, pop, and rock fans.

book Dylan had written the previous year, was scheduled to be published then as well.

Dylan liked to ride a big Triumph motorcycle on the winding roads in the Woodstock area. Early in the morning of July 29, 1966, he roared up the top of a hill and found himself blinded by the sun. "I went blind for a second and I kind of panicked or something. I stomped down on the brake and the rear wheel locked up on me and I went flyin'."

Dylan went to the hospital and emerged wearing a neck brace. He spent time recuperating at a local doctor's house before returning to his own. He canceled his heavy schedule of concerts and spent the rest of the year relaxing with Sara and the kids in Woodstock. "I was straining pretty hard and couldn't have gone on living that way much longer," he said. The accident wasn't exactly a blessing, but it did give him a chance to rest and think about what he wanted to do with his life and career. Dylan spent considerable time with his family, and many people in Woodstock thought of him as a family man as well as a musician-songwriter.

Dylan was back at work by spring 1967, though at an easier pace and without public performances. He and the Band began meeting that winter and recording songs at a house they called "Big Pink" in nearby Saugerties, New York. Soon, fans got hold of the tapes from those informal sessions and began passing them around.

The informal recordings were known as "bootlegs." Dylan and other musicians ordinarily didn't receive payments from bootlegs, and the quality of such recordings was usually far worse than commercial records. But bootlegs were very popular among fans. Bootlegs of Dylan concerts were traded and sold on the black market for years. (A small portion of the Big Pink songs were collected and officially released as the album *The Basement Tapes* in June 1975.)

The Country Sound

On October 3, 1967, Woody Guthrie died. Dylan, who still hadn't appeared publicly since his accident more than a year before, suggested a concert at Carnegie Hall in New York City to honor his idol. Since he suggested the concert, he couldn't very well refuse to perform in it.

Dylan and the Band returned to the stage January 20, 1968, with a host of folk performers as part of the large concert to honor Guthrie. Dylan played Guthrie songs, giving them a gentle rocking style with his acoustic guitar while the Band played behind him.

That very week, a new Dylan album was climbing the sales charts. Called *John Wesley Harding* after one of its songs, the album's music harked back to old country music roots. It blended country with rock and folk in the same way his earlier works blended folk with rock. Dylan used an acoustical guitar as a lead instrument, accompanied by an easygoing

bass and snare drum. The words spoke of common people and folk heroes, including Thomas Paine, a hero of the American Revolution. Dylan told stories in the songs, but tried to suggest ideas by leaving gaps. He wanted listeners to supply parts of the stories for themselves. This, he thought, would make the stories more interesting. "Anything we can imagine is really there," he said, referring to the stories the songs told.

Dylan spent much of early 1968 in Woodstock with Sara and the children. On June 5, his father died of a heart attack, and Dylan flew alone back to Hibbing for the funeral. He spent the night in his father's bedroom. At the funeral, he broke down.

Lay, Lady, Lay

Dylan continued his turn to country music in late 1968 and early 1969, working on a new album with some of the best country musicians. The most famous was country music star

Johnny Cash, whom Dylan had known for several years. The album was named *Nashville Skyline.* (Many consider Nashville, Tennessee, the unofficial capital of country music. Many country musicians record albums and perform there.)

Before *Nashville Skyline* was released, rock and roll and country were considered very different kinds of music, just as folk and rock had been. But country music had influenced Dylan when he was young, and it was very close to folk music. Cash had combined rock rhythms and styles with his own music. He had also been a fan of Dylan's since the *Freewheelin'* album. "I thought he was one of the best country singers I had ever heard," said Cash. "I always felt a lot in common with him."

Dylan performs with country music legend Johnny Cash in 1969. The two artists greatly respected each other's work, and both experimented with fusing rock and country sounds. Cash appeared on Dylan's *Nashville Skyline* as a special guest artist. He also wrote the liner notes for the album.

In the summer of 1969, the generation that came of age in reached a high point of celebration at a concert in Upstate New York. Known as Woodstock—though actually held more than an hour's drive away in Sullivan County—the festival celebrated peace, free love, and rock and roll. It came at the height of the hippie movement, and though Dylan was not listed on the program, many thought he might attend anyway, especially since the Band was playing there.

But Dylan had actually set out for England with his wife Sara (who was pregnant) and their children. "I didn't want to be part of that thing," he later told an interviewer. "The flower generation [hippies]—is that what it was? I wasn't into that at all. I just thought it was a lot of kids out and around wearin' flowers in their hair and takin' a lot of acid [LSD]. I mean what can you think about that?"

Dylan may not have wanted to exploit Woodstock or be connected to the flower generation. But he did perform at a large festival on the Isle of Wight a few days later. This concert became known as Great Britain's Woodstock.

THE WOODSTOCK MUSIC FESTIVAL, 1969

Dylan and his wife Sara in 1969. Critics who disliked Dylan's *Nashville Skyline* speculated that his contented family life was ruining his edge and negatively affecting his songwriting.

"Lay, Lady, Lay," a single from the new album, immediately rocketed up the charts. Besides the musical style, Dylan's voice on the album sounded very different. He said this was because he had stopped smoking cigarettes. Others believed that he had simply gone back to the inflections and voice he had used before becoming immersed in the folk scene.

Once again, some people criticized Dylan for this new direction. Some people called the songs on *Nashville Skyline* "hollow." Others even suggested that Dylan's happy family life was negatively affecting his abilities. But Dylan kept experimenting.

New Morning

In June 1970, Dylan released an album called *Self Portrait.* Like the 1962 album *Bob Dylan,* almost all the songs on the album were written by other performers. Critics wondered why Dylan was singing other people's songs. The album wasn't popular with fans and didn't sell well.

Dylan went back to his own songs and won back the critics with *New Morning* in October 1970. "We've got Dylan back again," proclaimed a headline in *Rolling Stone* magazine, the most influential rock and cultural magazine of the time. *New Morning* combined folk-style ballads with rock and roll. There were no protest songs or sharp rockers this time, and the sound couldn't be called country music at all. "Three Angels" and "Father of Night" have a directly religious feel. "Father of Night" could easily be a prayer. The songs were direct and immediate.

But Dylan's life was anything but simple or quiet. He had decided to break with his longtime manager Albert Grossman. He was also having conflicts with his record company and was determined not to release any more albums under his present contract. Partly because of this, he dropped out of public view. For much of 1971 and 1972, Dylan seemed to have retired. He bought a ranch in Tucson, Arizona, and spent a great deal of time there. The fact that he was no longer touring made some fans hungry for information about him. But it encouraged others to think he was no longer an important performer. After all, most pop groups enjoy only a few years in the spotlight. Dylan had been popular for nearly a decade. After capturing the spirit of a youthful generation, some thought Dylan's art would fade as that generation grew older.

But Dylan wasn't thinking of retiring. He still wrote songs that were as personal as any he had done. He wrote "Forever Young," a heartfelt celebration of life, for his son Jakob. In the winter of 1972, Dylan went down to Mexico for the filming of *Pat Garrett and Billy the Kid.* He had only a minor role in the movie, but he wrote music for it, including a song called "Knockin' on Heaven's Door." In the song, he gave voice to a tired lawman who had reached the end of the road.

Dylan played the bit part of Alias in director Sam Peckinpah's *Pat Garrett and Billy the Kid (below).* More notable than the film and Dylan's acting in it was Dylan's sound track.

Dylan himself was feeling new energy. The movie didn't do well at the box office, and legal problems delayed a sound track album. But "Knockin' on Heaven's Door" shot up the charts when it came out as a single. Working on the movie renewed Dylan's interest in film, and he began planning to make his own movie. He also decided to tour and perform in public again.

Dylan performs to a the sold-out Chicago Stadium in 1974. In just over a decade, Dylan had become a music icon for fans of folk, pop, and rock and roll.

chapter five
BLOOD
on the TRACKS

The crowd in Chicago Stadium, a large enclosed arena, slapped their hands together the night of January 3, 1974. They wanted Dylan and the Band. The metal rafters vibrated as the crowd of 18,500 chanted. Dylan planned to appear onstage before a mass audience for the first time in years, and they were anxious to see him.

When Bob Dylan finally strode out and began to play with the Band, the applause drowned out the sound system. Dylan launched into "Hero Blues," a song he'd written more than a decade earlier, but never released. He did the song in a new way with completely new words, and the crowd loved it. Dylan sang about a hero walking down a highway, and he was obviously referring to himself. He was back on the road, determined to see where it would take him.

That night and on the tour, he mixed old and new songs, acoustic folk and rock and roll. The protest songs Dylan mixed into the show seemed just as idealistic and fresh as when he had first written them.

Still, times had changed dramatically in the twelve years since Dylan had released his first album. As the baby boom generation (those who were among the sharp increase in births from 1946 to 1964) grew older, most of its members had stopped marching for civil rights and peace. Traditional concerns, such as raising families and moving ahead in careers, were more important to most of Dylan's fans. More than a few liked to listen to Dylan's music because it reminded them of the days when they were young and filled with hope and fresh ideas. But Dylan was looking ahead, not back.

Blood on the Tracks

As always, ideas for new songs poured into Dylan's mind. The road, the idea of the traveling performer, poets such as Rimbaud (a nineteenth-century French poet and traveler), even tarot cards used for fortune-telling—everything jumbled together as he worked ideas into songs. As before, Dylan shaped songs into short stories and imagined the singer as a character. Love and its many phases and moods was a constant theme. Some songs about love's pain were sad. This wasn't an accident. Dylan's marriage was rocky, and rumors persisted that he had been seeing other women.

The conflicting thoughts and emotions about his family and love life found their way into his music. In "Tangled Up in Blue," for example, the singer goes to New Orleans, Louisiana, where he meets a woman who seems to have been his lover in a different lifetime. In "Idiot Wind," the narrator wanders across America trying to understand love and human suffering, only to discover that he never will.

Dylan included these songs on the 1975 album *Blood on the Tracks*. Most, though not all, critics and fans immediately recognized the record as one of Dylan's masterworks. The music was varied and exciting. The writing was some of Dylan's best. He created precise pictures with sharp details.

Born, perhaps, of pain and strife in his marriage, *Blood on the Tracks* is considered by many fans and critics to be Dylan's best work for its soulful lyrics and music. With the album completed in 1974, Dylan hired new backup musicians to rerecord five songs for the record. *Blood on the Tracks* was released in January 1975.

As he had in the past, he managed to suggest longer stories by choosing his words carefully and leaving things out that listeners could fill in with their imaginations. In "Lily, Rosemary and the Jack of Hearts," for example, Dylan told a story that could have filled a two-hour movie. But he used only forty-eight sentences.

Hard Rain

In July 1975, Ramblin' Jack Elliott came back to New York City for some gigs at the Other End, a popular Greenwich Village club that featured folk music. Elliott, with his trademark cowboy hat and easygoing style, found an enthusiastic audience for his music and quickly got into a groove. The audience listened enthusiastically, clapping and howling for more. Then as he paused and started to tell the audience about his next song, someone joined him onstage. It was Bob Dylan, who had just come into town himself. The folk standard "Pretty Boy Floyd" turned into an unexpected duet between the two old friends.

They shared the stage for a few numbers, and the show became more Dylan's than Ramblin' Jack's.

Dylan had gone to the city to attend a Rolling Stones concert, renew musical friendships, and check out the local scene. He had several ideas simmering, but they hadn't quite jelled. Over the next few weeks, he hooked up with other musicians as an idea began to take shape for a new tour.

The Band had decided to end their touring days. Dylan not only wanted to get back on the road but also wanted to find a new sound. "Bob was trying to find a situation where he could make music with new people," said rock guitarist Eric Clapton, a longtime friend. "He was just driving around, picking up musicians, and bringing them back to the [recording and jam] sessions."

Among those he recruited was a violinist named Scarlet Rivera. Dylan had never played onstage with a violin before. (The instrument, often called a fiddle, is important in some traditional folk music.) Dylan also ran into a friend, director Jacques Levy, at the Other End. Levy, who had written songs with Roger McGuinn of the Byrds, was a psychologist and theater director. One night Dylan suggested to Levy that they go to his loft apartment and work on a song. Over the next few weeks, the two men worked together on a dozen or so tunes, including Dylan's first protest song in many years, "Hurricane Carter." The song told of the unjust conviction of Rubin "Hurricane" Carter for murder in New Jersey. It became a well-known single and the opening song for *Desire,* Dylan's fifteenth original album, released later in 1975.

The album also included a love song called "Sara," dedicated to his wife. The two had had many disagreements, partly because Dylan was rumored to be seeing other women. In the song, Dylan remembered their love and asked her not to leave

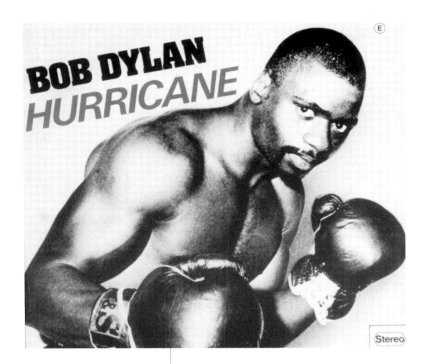

him. He sang the song for her one night shortly after he wrote it, and their love once more grew strong.

Rolling Thunder

Dylan and Levy hatched an idea to tour the United States, doing shows mostly at small clubs like New York's Other End. In Dylan's mind, the tour would be like a roaming jam session or informal musical party. Musicians at jam sessions often improvise and experiment with new sounds. The tour ended up being just that, with a little bit of circus sideshow thrown in. Dylan filmed some of the shows for a movie he was making called *Renaldo and Clara*. The clips show people having a lot of fun joking and fooling around behind the scenes.

Musically, some of the shows were great successes. Others were not. Dylan was a big reason. "He'd just wander off somewhere, expecting us to follow him," said Mick Ronson, one of the musicians on the tour. Dylan often tried completely different versions of his songs at performances. For example, he had become interested in reggae, a musical style from Jamaica that featured very prominent percussion and deliberate beats. He added a reggae sound to "Isis," a song from *Desire,* then a few days later changed the arrangement so it sounded almost as if it were a heavy metal tune with wailing guitars.

On the whole, fans seemed to appreciate the energy Dylan and the variety of musicians brought to the shows each night. Shows ran four or even five hours, and fans found something to appreciate at every performance. Among the musicians on tour was folksinger Joan Baez. She had not played with Dylan for nearly a decade.

Joan Baez was a typical thirteen-year-old high school student in 1954, when folksinger Pete Seeger came to her school to perform. By the end of the show, she was determined to follow in his musical footsteps.

Born on Staten Island, New York, on January 9, 1941, Baez has a rich, haunting voice. Like Seeger, she learned to accompany herself on an acoustic guitar.

After graduating from high school, she went to Boston University in Massachusetts. She was soon singing in local coffeehouses for five dollars a night. The next spring, she was an instant hit at the 1959 Newport Folk Festival. Her 1960 solo album, *Joan Baez,* brought her national fame, and she was soon selling out concerts in big U.S. cities.

Baez's mother and father were Quakers, and they raised their daughter to believe in nonviolence and fairness for all. Baez applied these important principles to her own life. She sang songs protesting racial inequality and appeared at fund-raising events to help causes she believed in.

THE MUSIC OF JOAN BAEZ

Baez met Bob Dylan in April 1961 in New York. The two fell in love and began to sing at each other's concerts. Baez also included some of Dylan's songs on her albums, helping him become much better known.

Although their love affair ended bitterly in 1965, their musical friendship lasted much longer. Baez joined Dylan on his *Rolling Thunder Revue* tour of 1975. Critics say the title song of her 1975 best-selling album, *Diamonds and Rust,* referred to their love affair. It is a sad song about how love fades away.

Baez has recorded more than thirty albums since 1959. In addition, she has earned six Grammy Award nominations.

It is possible to hear what Baez and Dylan sounded like in concert by listening to their duets on *Bob Dylan Live 1964: Concert at Philharmonic Hall (The Bootleg Series, Vol. 6),* which was recorded at the height of their love affair. Baez's contributions to the *Rolling Thunder Revue* tour are included on *Bob Dylan: Live 1975 (The Bootleg Series, Vol. 5).*

Dylan took a break from touring and directing to perform with his former backup group the Band during the group's farewell concert, The Last Waltz, on Thanksgiving Day 1976.

Disappointments

Sara joined Dylan on the tour, but their marriage once more faltered. They disagreed over many things, including a home they built in California. Dylan's career added extra stress, and he spent much time away from Sara and the children. But his attraction to other women was probably the biggest problem in their marriage. Sara filed for divorce on March 1, 1977. A child custody battle followed.

In the songs Dylan wrote in the 1970s, women sometimes appeared as goddesses with magical powers. But in his personal life, Dylan often saw women as sexual objects.

He seems to have had an emotional need to be close to women. At the same time, he felt a need to move on to something, or someone, new. Most of his affairs ended quickly. Even so, Dylan provided money to many of his ex-lovers and continued to support his children.

On August 16, 1977, Elvis Presley died. Known as the king of rock and roll, Elvis was the first great white rock star of the 1950s. The news shook Dylan. Like many, he was saddened to learn that Elvis's life had degenerated into a drug-filled haze as his career passed its prime.

Dylan's own career had headed downward. *Renaldo and Clara,* the movie he had been working on during the

Dylan, as Renaldo, opposite his wife Sara, as Clara, in a scene from his film *Renaldo and Clara.* The film follows Renaldo's quest for meaning in the world and in the music scene set against actual *Rolling Thunder* concert footage.

Released in 1978 at four hours long, *Renaldo and Clara*'s perplexing plot and self-indulgent content left moviegoers confused and disappointed. Faring far better than *Renaldo and Clara* that year was director Martin Scorsese's *The Last Waltz*, a documentary of the Band, featuring Bob Dylan and others. The film instantly became a classic.

Rolling Thunder Revue and *Hard Rain* tours, was released in early 1978. The movie combined concert performances with scenes that seem to be taken from a fairy tale or ancient legend. Characters appeared and disappeared, sometimes changing into other characters. The story line was baffling. Dylan spent months editing and choosing from more than one hundred hours of film. But critics gave it terrible reviews, saying it didn't make any sense.

Following the movie, Dylan released an album called *Street Legal.* Horns and stringed instruments accompanied many of the songs as Dylan took yet another new direction. But the music failed to get many people excited. Reviewers said the songs were not as good as his earlier ones, and the album did not sell well. While a tour in Europe attracted good crowds and positive reviews, Dylan's reputation had slipped in the United States.

The 1960s were long gone. The world had changed, and more and more, it seemed that Bob Dylan, rather than being a step or two ahead, was falling behind. Some writers were starting to compare him to Elvis—and not in a good way.

Dylan opens the European leg of his 1978 world tour in London, England. Already on the road several months, Dylan had a month of engagements in Europe. But the longest part of the tour—three months in North America—lay in front of him.

chapter six
SAVED

Dylan took a breath as the band finished the song. He was in San Diego, California, on November 17, 1978. He'd been on the road for months, and his body felt worn down. His voice had started to run thin.

Someone in the crowd threw something up toward the edge of the stage. Dylan ordinarily ignored that sort of thing, but for some unknown reason, he walked over and picked it up. It was a silver cross.

Dylan thought little about the cross until a few nights later, in Tucson, Arizona. Sitting alone in his hotel room, he felt another presence in the room. Then he had a vision of Jesus Christ.

At that moment, the Jewish guy became a born-again Christian. "Jesus put his hand on me. It was a physical thing. I felt it. I felt it all over me," Dylan said later. "I felt my whole body tremble. The glory of the Lord knocked me down and picked me up."

Slow Train

Dylan had always used religious images and themes in his songs. But during his career as a songwriter and performer, he had never been very devout or outwardly religious. He had been raised as a Jew and knew Hebrew, the ancient language used in Jewish scriptures. But suddenly, he believed that Jesus Christ was the son of God. As a born-again Christian, he believed that Jesus Christ was his personal savior and inspiration. Dylan read the New Testament of the Bible for inspiration. He not only went to church but attended Bible school for three months, studying texts and learning about Christianity.

Dylan believed that the apocalypse, or the end of the world, was coming. "We're living in the end times," he said, and he said so in his songs. He turned out an album of religious songs called *Slow Train Coming,* named after a song on the album. The song spoke of God's judgment. In some ways, the idea behind "Slow Train Coming" was very similar to the ideas in "Hard Rain," except that the words were religious.

The critical reaction to the new album was split. Many people recognized that the songs were among the best Dylan had written in years. The words were vivid, and the emotion was strong. Top-notch musicians played with him and their work was very good. The music included a horn section and backup singers. Dylan had used these before, but he had never found a pleasing balance between the style and his words. On this album, they blended perfectly, but many listeners didn't like the message in the songs. "Bob Dylan has never seemed more perfect and more impressive than on this album," wrote critic Charles Shaar Murray. "He has also never seemed more unpleasant and hate filled."

Slow Train became a commercial success, and it also appealed to a new audience of committed Christians, many of whom were too young to have experienced Dylan before. At his concerts, he mixed traditional gospel—performed by his backup singers—with songs from the album and some of his new pieces. Typically, his concerts did not include songs from before *Slow Train*. Dylan felt that he could not relate to those songs because he had become a different person.

After becoming a born-again Christian, Dylan released the album *Slow Train Coming* in August 1979. With a clear religious theme, *Slow Train* included the songs "Precious Angel," "Gonna Change My Way of Thinking," and "When He Returns." Despite the album's religious overtones, its title track (song), as well as its first track, "Gotta Serve Somebody," received extensive play on pop and rock radio.

Many old fans were disappointed. Some walked out of the concerts. Others heckled him. When fans chanted for the old songs, Dylan sometimes ignored them—and sometimes preached to them.

Eager fans camp outside a U.S. ticket office to get Dylan tickets in the late 1970s. While Dylan still drew a number of devoted fans, his religious zeal kept others away.

"'The lamb of God which taketh away the sins of the world,'" he said, quoting from the Bible. "I wonder how many of you people understand that?" Sometimes he lost his temper onstage. In Arizona one night, the crowd began chanting for "rock and roll."

"You still wanna rock and roll?" he thundered at them. "I'll tell you what the two kinds of people are. Don't matter how much money you got, there's only two kinds of people: there's saved people and there's lost people. Yeah. Remember that I told you that. You may never see me again. You may not see me, but somewhere down the line you remember you heard it here, that Jesus is Lord. Every knee shall bow down!"

Criticism

Dylan had long ago proved that he would do what he felt he had to do no matter how many people booed. He believed that he had to spread the message of the coming Armageddon, the final battle between good and evil, and Jesus' power to redeem souls. Again and again, he faced hostile audiences. Gradually, the audiences learned that he would play his new material no matter what they did. Those who didn't like it stayed away. Others who did like it—or at least weren't bothered by it—came to listen. During his last concerts in Ohio, the fans seemed more appreciative. Dylan stopped preaching between songs and even added an extra number at the end.

Dylan wrote more Christian songs for his next album, *Saved.* With the help of his gospel-singing backup singers and rock-and-roll band, Dylan made the songs seem a little closer to those from a live performance than the *Slow Train* songs. In choosing titles such as "Pressing On" and "Are You Ready?" Dylan clearly stated his religious beliefs and encouraged others to believe in Jesus Christ. The album sold very poorly. His next album, *Shot of Love,* was still Christian-oriented, but on a more personal level. Dylan took a step back from direct preaching and worked his beliefs into stories. But the album did even worse than *Saved.*

Punk and Post-Punk

The end of the 1970s and beginning of the 1980s saw new shifts in popular music. By then most of the major rock bands of the 1960s had stopped performing. New musical forms had gained popularity. Disco, a mixture of soft rock, jazz, and soul music, was popular in dance clubs. Rap music, with its driving bass beat and spoken lyrics, was just starting to be performed on the streets of big cities in the United States. Meanwhile, some young rockers were taking up a new form of rock music called punk.

Dylan appreciated the raw, youthful energy of punk bands, such as the Sex Pistols *(above)*. While Dylan would not turn to performing punk, its unpolished honesty would influence his songwriting.

Punk rock featured bitter lyrics and loud, often harsh-sounding guitars. Punk rock bands tended to be small, with a drum, two guitars, and little else. In some ways, punk was a reaction to the sweet, polished sounds of disco and soft rock. In other ways, it was a return to rock and roll's roots, celebrating youthful rebellion and political concerns as sixties rockers did. Popularized by British bands such as the Sex Pistols and later the Clash, punk spread to the United States.

Bob Dylan was not a punk rocker, but he had heard and liked the music. The new sounds began running through his head, and gradually, Dylan rounded up a new set of musicians rooted in the new style. The album that resulted was *Infidels*. The album's music was not punk rock, but it did mark another break for Dylan. Though still clearly influenced by religion, the songs were much less preachy than *Slow Train* and *Saved*. Some contained references to the Jewish Old Testament, and one song, "Neighborhood Bully," celebrated Israel.

Critics liked *Infidels* much better than Dylan's previous two albums. Once again he had reinvented himself. When he toured Europe in 1984, he did something he hadn't done in quite awhile. He mixed in songs from the 1960s, sometimes changing the words, sometimes not. Meanwhile, songs from the Christian albums slipped out of his sets.

Though some punk bands would parody him, Dylan's punk influences were clearly evident on his gritty *Infidels*, released in November 1983. Fans and critics embraced the album and hailed it as Dylan's return to rock and roll. Four outtakes—tracks Dylan chose not to included on *Infidels*—appear on *The Bootleg Series, Vol. 1–3*.

Eventually, he wrote lines in a song called "A Tight Connection to My Heart," which seemed to say that he no longer believed in Jesus Christ as deeply as he had. As the eighties continued, Dylan drew closer to his Jewish roots.

One remnant of his Christian period stayed with him in the eighties. Since the 1970s, Dylan had dated one of his former backup singers, an African American woman named Carolyn Dennis. On January 31, 1986, she had a child named Desiree. The girl's birth was kept secret. He married Carolyn in June 1986, also in secret.

RECORDS AND CDS

We have many ways of listening to music. We might buy a CD or download songs from the Internet. But in the 1960s and early 1970s, neither CDs nor the Internet existed. In fact, most people didn't even have stereos when Dylan's first albums were released. "I listened to the first seven Dylan albums [through *Blonde on Blonde*] in mono, on a record player vintage 1958," remembered Peter Knobler, a magazine reviewer in 1973. Most early Dylan fans heard the music the same way. Records were thin plastic discs. The sound came from a needle that responded to the grooves in the record. This method could produce high-quality sounds, but on most record players, the sound was muddy and indistinct. The needle wore down the record, and this distorted the sound after the record was played a few times.

CDs started to replace records in the 1980s. While CDs are not perfect, they last longer and produce better sound than records on less expensive equipment. In addition, even inexpensive modern digital sound systems can reproduce a richer, truer sound than the units of the 1960s.

Dylan performs with Tom Petty in 1986. Married that year, Dylan also went on the road with Tom Petty and the Heartbreakers for the group's *True Confessions* tour, sharing a double bill.

One reason for the secrecy was the craziness of some of Dylan's fans. According to biographer Howard Sounes, Dylan's staff kept a list of five hundred people considered potentially dangerous to him. Two women followed him around on tour, claiming to be his wife. "Most fans were perfectly sane, of course," writes Sounes, "but there were many who could not resist trying to make contact with Dylan offstage, and would follow his tour buses along the freeways and search out his hotels."

Commercial Success

While Dylan's new albums were not the top sellers his earlier ones had been, they still sold decently. Between touring and album sales, he became rich. He bought many properties, including a farm in Minnesota, north of Minneapolis along the Crow River, and a house in Malibu, California, overlooking the beach. There he could retreat from his busy career. He might wear raggedy clothes, but the person who once called himself a vagabond was a millionaire.

"The myth of the starving artist is a myth," said Dylan. "The big bankers and prominent young ladies who buy art started it. They just want to keep the artist under their thumb. Who says an artist can't have money?"

Though looking the hardened, starving musician-artist in this late 1980s promotional photo, Dylan was a wealthy man and was unashamed to admit it. He had come a long way from his years of imitating what he—and others—thought a folksinger and rock musician should be.

What do you get when you take five famous rock stars, put them in a garage, and ask them to fill a blank spot on an upcoming album? You get the most star-studded garage band of all time, the Traveling Wilburys.

In rock music, the term *garage band* means a not-yet famous band that practices at someone's house—often in a garage. In this case, the band may not have been famous, but its members were. George Harrison had been a member of the Beatles and had played on his own since the band broke up at the end of the 1960s. Roy Orbison was a ground-breaking musician who had been playing country-blues-infused rock since the late 1950s. Jeff Lynne played with the Electric Light Orchestra, a 1970s group that popularized the use of synthesizers and other electronically generated sounds. Tom Petty was known for punk-infused rock as the front man for Tom Petty and the Heartbreakers. And Bob Dylan was Bob Dylan.

It all started when Harrison asked Lynne to drop what he was doing to help produce a track for a new CD. Lynne was working with Orbison and Petty on different albums.

THE TRAVELING WILBURYS

Both volunteered to help. Harrison called Dylan to ask if they could use Dylan's private studio, which was located in a corner of his garage. Dylan agreed and even offered to provide refreshments.

Soon after the famous musicians arrived, Harrison teased Dylan into helping him write some lyrics for a song he was struggling with. Within a few hours, they had finished and recorded the song. The producers liked it and suggested an entire album. They wrote an album's worth of songs during the summer barbecues and then recorded them in ten days.

Still having fun, the musicians decided to invent a name for the band, pretending they were unknown. Harrison came up with the name *Wilbury*. Whenever something went wrong in the studio, he would blame it on invisible gremlins he nicknamed "wilburys." Dylan was Lucky Wilbury; Orbison was Lefty Wilbury; Petty called himself Charlie T. Jr.; Harrison was Nelson Wilbury; and Lynne was Otis Wilbury. The 1988 album, *The Traveling Wilburys, Vol. 1* was a big seller and won a Grammy Award for Best Rock Performance by a Duo or Group.

But while most fans would agree that Dylan deserved the money he earned, many were saddened when he allowed "The Times They Are A-Changin'" to be used as an advertisement, first for a Canadian bank and then for Coopers & Lybrand LLP, one of the largest accounting firms in the world. Fans considered the song an important work of art and a piece of their own past. Fans thought Dylan was selling out. "When the song was written, it was about social justice and the change of institutions," said a spokesperson for Coopers & Lybrand. "It's still an important song, but it's about different things today."

After a tour with Tom Petty, a few mediocre new albums, and a television commercial, some critics and fans in the late 1980s wondered if Dylan *(above)* had become a sellout and a mere "oldies" act.

An Oldies Act?

Dylan had gone through different periods when he refused to play his older songs. When he began playing them regularly again in the 1980s, most fans were pleased. But some critics thought he was saying that his new material was not as good or as important as his 1960s music had been. They pointed out that the songs he was writing were not breaking new ground. His sound was of the eighties, not ahead of it.

Dylan's career had entered a new phase. In the 1960s and 1970s, Dylan was seen as a prophet of change in society and in music. If he was no longer a prophet, could he be just a performer? His old songs were great, but were they all going to be recycled as television jingles? Was Bob Dylan about to become just another golden oldies act?

Dylan plays with the Grateful Dead at the Meadowlands arena in New Jersey on July 10, 1987. After six unsatisfying shows with the Dead that summer, Dylan was wondering if he should pack it in.

chapter seven
GRATEFUL
but not DEAD

The crowd streaming into Giants Stadium at the Meadowlands in New Jersey looked like typical hippies. They wore long hair, colorful tie-dyed clothes, sandals and love beads. Many were high or "stoned" on illegal drugs or alcohol. It was a typical 1960s rock concert, but the year was 1987. Bob Dylan had joined forces with the Grateful Dead, a legendary band whose fans were more fanatical than his own.

For a good part of the show, Dylan led the Dead through rambling renditions of some of his better-known classics. It was part jam and part free-for-all. At times he seemed to forget many of the words to his own songs. Many in the crowd were in awe of Dylan and the Grateful Dead. But Dylan seemed overwhelmed in the massive setting, and the show was not very good. Dylan did not like to rehearse, and this made the songs sound sloppy. Also, the stadium made the music hard to hear and distorted the sound. Dylan and the Dead put on six stadium shows that summer. They introduced many new fans to Dylan's music, but the shows were not artistic successes.

During the fall, Dylan played in Israel and then Europe. Reporters noted that he was downing several mixed drinks each night, often before shows. But the problem was more than just alcohol, and even Dylan realized it. He had been a star for nearly thirty years. The glimmer had faded. Dylan had always been seen as something more than just another singer. He was a poet-singer who knew exactly what was going on in society and could somehow give it voice, even before most people realized what "it" was. But he'd lost that ability. Sometimes it seemed that he couldn't even connect to his old songs. "I'd kind of reached the end of the line. Whatever I'd started out to do, it wasn't that. I was going to pack it in," he said.

Bringing It All Back Home

Dylan kept trying to connect, like a baseball batter in the middle of a slump trying to find his swing. He played different songs from his vast songbook. He spent hours jamming and learning traditional pieces from musicians such as the Dead's bandleader and guitarist Jerry Garcia. And he kept playing and touring.

On October 5, 1987, Dylan found himself onstage in Locarno, Switzerland. Something happened that he couldn't really describe or even understand. But it filled him with new energy. "It all just came to me. All of a sudden I could sing anything," he said later. "I can't really retire now because I haven't done anything yet. . . . I want to see where this [playing music and his life in general] will lead me, because now I can control it."

Dylan's concerts began to improve that fall. His singing sounded better. He paid more attention to his guitar work. Once more he started looking in new directions, playing with different musicians, including jazz musician David Bromberg.

One of the most recent developments for Dylan as well as the rest of the music industry has been the release of rare recordings from the files or "vaults" of old tapes kept by the record company. In 1991 Sony Music—which had taken over Columbia and its parent, CBS Records—released a three-CD set called *Bob Dylan: The Bootleg Series, Vol. 1–3* with previously unreleased songs from 1961 to 1991.

THE BOOTLEG SERIES

The recording company has since released tapes of some of Dylan's live performances from 1966, 1975, and 1964. There is much, much more material in the vaults, including an album's worth of recordings from the period of *Slow Train Coming* and *Saved* that Dylan prepared for an unreleased album. Each installment in the *Bootleg Series* has generated excitement and nostalgia from fans.

And then in 1992, Dylan jumped in an unusual direction—backward. Not back into his own past, but into American folk song history. He released an album of classic songs called *Good as I Been to You*. Dylan's raspy voice worked well with ballads such as "Frankie & Albert," a song about a woman who killed her lover after he "done her wrong." He had fun rollicking with the comic "Froggie Went a Courtin'," a fairytale song about a frog marrying a mouse. The album dove into the deep, strong currents of traditional American folk music. The next year, 1993, Dylan released another album of old songs, these more blues-oriented, called *World Gone Wrong*.

Far from washed up in the early 1990s, a renewed Dylan toured and released albums. He even played President Bill Clinton's inauguration *(below)*.

The simple, moving vocals showed how important the folk tradition was. "Two Soldiers," for example, told a story about the American Civil War and what it felt like to fight in it. In roughly six

Recorded in January 1997, Dylan's *Time Out of Mind* was released September 30 of that year. Many fans and critics agreed that *Time out of Mind* was Dylan's finest work since *Blood on the Tracks* (1966) and *Blonde on Blonde* (1975).

minutes, the words and melody told listeners what historians try to communicate in a four-hundred-page book.

In sales, the two albums couldn't compare to those of Dylan's early career. But the music was some of the best he had made in years. Some of his best guitar picking was featured on the two CDs. Nearly six decades of life's ups and downs echoed through his voice as he sang the traditional music. The songs seemed to come from his soul.

Out of Mind and Heart

Dylan changed directions once more in his next album, *Time Out of Mind,* released in 1997. The recording sessions involved a wide range of musicians, and the songs varied sharply. The finished product combined modern rock sounds and the smoother, thicker tone of rock music from the late fifties.

But before the album could be released, the fifty-six-year-old Dylan checked into a Los Angeles hospital with a serious ailment. A fungal infection called histoplasmosis infected his lungs, making it difficult for him to breathe properly.

The disease also put severe pressure on his heart. Dylan was so weak that he took about six weeks to recover. "The pain stopped me in my tracks and fried my mind," he said. "I was so sick, my mind just blanked out." A flood of newspaper stories proclaimed that Dylan was fighting for his life.

Biographer Clinton Heylin felt that Dylan's sickness caused many people to believe he would die. Because of that, critics and fans thought about Dylan's work and his place in music and in American culture. Whether or not his illness had a direct impact on the sales of *Time Out of Mind,* the album did very well when it was released in September 1997. It returned Dylan to the top of the pop charts. Critics also loved the songs. The album was nominated for three Grammy Awards—Best Contemporary Folk Album; Best Hard Rock, Male; and Album of the Year.

Dylan and actress Lauren Bacall after receiving 1997 Kennedy Center Honors for artistic contribution. Dylan's *Time Out of Mind* also was nominated for three Grammy Awards that year.

Dylan holds his Grammy Award for *Time Out of Mind,* the 1997 Album of the Year during the Fortieth Annual Grammy Awards in 1998. Dylan accepted two other Grammy Awards for the critically acclaimed album.

The Grammy nominations were not Dylan's only honors. He met with the pope and heads of state during the nineties, as many honored him for his achievements. On December 7, 1997, Dylan went to Washington to receive one of the highest honors awarded to the country's artists, the Kennedy Center Honor. During a ceremony at the State Department, Dylan received a three-minute standing ovation.

On February 25, 1998, *Time Out of Mind* won all three of the awards for which it had been nominated. The wide range of the awards said as much about Dylan's importance as the album itself. In his acceptance speech, Dylan thanked his producers and fellow musicians. He also spoke in awe of seeing early rock-and-roll star Buddy Holly when Dylan was sixteen or seventeen. The man who had become bigger than any other rock and roller still vividly remembered the moments in his youth that had inspired him.

Onward

Though Dylan did not speak to reporters about his mother, he and Bea remained fairly close through the years. In January 2000, she passed away, and he returned to Duluth to bury her. As usual, though, he kept his deepest feelings mostly to himself. "He doesn't talk a lot," noted a friend. "You can only know that he would be sad."

In 2001 Dylan released an album called *Love and Theft.* The first song, "Tweedle Dee & Tweedle Dum," got the collection off to a running start with a rock-country beat. The album seemed to build on the style Dylan used in *Time Out of Mind.* The songs had a happier, lighter feel than the earlier album. The subjects were personal. The songwriter sang about things that had happened or were happening to him.

Over the years, critics have praised young folksingers and rock musicians by calling them "the new Dylan." In the 1990s, a new Dylan really appeared on the rock scene: Bob Dylan's son Jakob.

Born in December 1969, Jakob is the fourth son of Bob and Sara Dylan. Jakob spent his childhood in Los Angeles and New York. The Dylans kept their children away from the music scene so they could have a normal childhood.

But by the time Jakob was in his twenties, he had struck out on his own as a singer and songwriter. He started the band the Wallflowers with some friends. In 1992 the band released its first CD, *The Wallflowers.* Four years later, with some new members but with Jakob still fronting the group, the Wallflowers struck gold with a second CD, *Bringing Down the Horse.* Released in 1996, the CD sold about six million copies and received four Grammy nominations. It won two—for Best Vocal Performance and Best Songwriting (for "One Headlight").

Jakob has worked hard on his own, and critics say he tried not to take advantage of his father's fame. But even at the Grammy's, he had to share the spotlight with his more famous father. Bob Dylan received three Grammy Awards that year, two for his album *Time Out of Mind* (Best Album and Best Contemporary Folk Album), and one for a song on the album, "Cold Irons Bound" (Best Male Rock Vocal Performance).

Jakob also writes songs for film and television. In 2003 his song "Empire in My Mind" for CBS's *The Guardian* received an American Society of Composers, Authors, and Publishers (ASCAP) Film and Television Music Award, a prestigious industry honor.

Jakob Dylan recalled in a November 2000 interview with the *Minneapolis Star Tribune* that his father didn't teach him directly how to play but that he learned a great deal simply by listening to records with him. He says he never shows his father any of his songs before they are recorded. He will, however, send rough versions of his recordings to his dad and some friends to get ideas and feedback.

JAKOB DYLAN AND THE WALLFLOWERS

When he had started his career, Dylan had strained his voice to sound like old folksingers. Later, the sound came naturally. Four decades of constant singing had worn down his voice. "Dylan compensates for his utterly ravaged voice by racing through songs instead of stretching and bending phrases as he once did," noted Greg Kot, a reviewer. But he still managed to find a way to express the emotion inherent in the words.

Although he was past sixty, Dylan remained for many a symbol of the 1960s. People often asked him for political statements, but he refused to endorse political parties. His own political feelings defied easy categories. "There is no right and there is no left," he told an interviewer. "There's truth and there's untruth, y'know. . . . Other people might have other ideas about things, but I don't, because I'm not that smart."

But he could still surprise people. In April 2004, he appeared in a television commercial for Victoria's Secret, a chain of women's clothing stores specializing in lingerie. In the commercial, he walks mysteriously through Venice, Italy, haunted by an angel wearing Victoria's Secret underwear. Part of his song, "Love Sick," from *Time Out of Mind,* plays in the background. The commercial drew a lot of attention because Dylan was in it. Many fans again accused him of selling out. Others were simply curious about why he would appear in it.

Where He Stands

By any measure, Bob Dylan is one of the most productive and successful artists in American music history. The sheer range of his music—from folk ballad to guitar-blazing rock to religious songs—is unmatched. His impact on twentieth-century popular music cannot be measured. He changed rock music and influenced all forms that flowed from it. His compositions and performances shaped folk, rock, and Christian rock.

Bob Dylan has released more than forty albums and written well over five hundred songs. His album and CD sales are approaching 100 million. Few artists in any field or genre have managed to combine creative genius with commercial success as Dylan has. This may have been due in part to the large generation of baby boomers who came of age in the 1960s. They were eager to hear music that celebrated their ideals, and they had the money to buy it. The mass media of television and radio spread Dylan's fame far and wide, fanning sales of his albums. But his commercial success and his genius worked together. He was not satisfied with being popular or making money. He kept pushing to top himself and to change. He loved to explore all sorts of music, old and new.

An autographed Dylan guitar *(below, right)* hangs with others to be auctioned during the early 2000s. The guitar's presence in the auction is evidence of Dylan's legendary status and ongoing popularity.

For his entire career, Bob Dylan has rewritten his past as well as his present. In 2004 he did it in book form, publishing *Chronicles, Volume One*. In this wide-ranging memoir, Dylan wrote for the first time at length about his musical roots in Minnesota, about coming to New York City in the early 1960s, and about hitting a creative bottom in 1987.

The book jumps around, touching on different parts of his career. At some points, it seems more a conversation than a book, a fascinating, informal insight into Dylan's thought process. While biographers have covered most of the incidents Dylan mentions, he adds details and a personal perspective that haven't been available before. For example, Dylan says his repertoire of old-style folk songs set him apart when he first started playing in Greenwich Village. "I'd either drive people away or they'd come in closer to see what it was all about," he writes. "There were a lot of better singers and better musicians around these places but there wasn't anybody close in nature to what I was doing. Folk songs were the way I explored the universe."

Because of the long length of Dylan's career, no book could sum it all up. He does not attempt to do that in *Chronicles, Volume One*. Much, though not all, of the book is about his career during the 1960s. In typical Dylan style, he leaves many questions unanswered. Fans and biographers looking for more insight into his career can only hope that the title's promise of more volumes to come is fulfilled.

CHRONICLES, VOLUME ONE

He put what he heard into his own songs. The success that he had already received made people pay attention to what he did. In his best songs, Bob Dylan voiced the emotions—the loves, fears, hopes, and dreams—of a generation. In his songs of true genius, he gave voice to timeless truths.

The seemingly immortal Dylan performs during the taping of country musician Willie Nelson's TV special "Willie Nelson and Friends: Outlaws and Angels" in 2004. That same year, Dylan teamed up with Nelson for a U.S. tour. In his sixties, Dylan continues to tour.

L I S T E N
BOB

The only way to really appreciate and come close to understanding any musician and his or her art is to listen to the music. Bob Dylan is no exception.

Every fan will recommend a different favorite starting point. Many say the best way to experience Dylan is just to pick any album and jump in. But several collections provide starting points. *Biograph* covers Dylan's career to the mid-1980s. It includes a few songs that were not included on the original album. The songs are not arranged in chronological order, but there are notes on the productions and an accompanying booklet.

A good introduction to the wide range of Dylan's music before 1971 are his two early collections of *Greatest Hits, Volume One* and *Volume Two.* The songs can give a new listener ideas on albums to check out next.

For an idea of how Dylan sounded in concert with the Band, check out the double CD set *Before the Flood. Bob Dylan Unplugged,* released in 1995 and containing several of the same songs, demonstrates how much—and in some cases how little—his sound changed in twenty years.

ING TO
DYLAN

The albums from *Blood on the Tracks* to *Under the Red Sky*—a span of nearly twenty years—are represented by *Greatest Hits, Volume Three*. Unfortunately, the span is so large it's impossible to get a full idea of Dylan's art during that period.

Anyone looking for an introduction to American folk music should check out the six-CD *American Folk Music* collection, compiled by Harry Smith. The collection, originally released by Folkways Records and Service Corp. in 1952, has been reissued by the Smithsonian and is available in different forms. It is often referred to as the "Harry Smith folk collection."

A good survey of performers connected with the 1960s folk revival can be found in the compilation, *Washington Square Memoirs—The Great Urban Folk Boom, 1950–1970*. The three-CD set was compiled by Rhino Records and released in 2001. It includes a booklet with excellent background on the revival.

For a survey of American musical styles—sometimes called "roots music"—check out the four-CD collection, *American Roots Music,* a companion to the PBS documentary series of the same name. The collection includes samples of jazz and other forms as well as folk.

Sources

p. 10   Robert Shelton, *No Direction Home: The Life and Music of Bob Dylan* (New York: William Morrow, 1986), 33.

p. 10   Ibid.

p. 10   Ibid.

p. 14   Clinton Heylin, *Bob Dylan: Behind the Shades Revisited* (New York: William Morrow, 2001), 16.

p. 15   Ibid., 17.

p. 15   Ibid.

p. 18   Miles, comp., *Bob Dylan in His Own Words* (New York: Omnibus Press, 1987), 19.

p. 18   Ibid.

p. 18   Heylin, 33.

p. 19   Ibid., 29.

p. 20   Shelton, 66.

p. 20   Ibid.

p. 28   Shelton, 95.

p. 29   Heylin, 62.

p. 29   Ibid.

p. 29   Ibid., 59.

p. 30   Shelton, 102.

p. 30   John Baldie, liner notes to *The Bootleg Series, Volumes 1–3,* CD (New York: Sony Music, 1991), 3.

p. 32   Paul J. Robbins, "Bob Dylan in His Own Words," in *The Bob Dylan Companion,* ed. Carl Benson (New York: Schirmer Books, 1998), 53.

p. 32   Bernard Kleinman, "Dylan on Dylan," in *Dylan Companion,* 33.

p. 32   Miles, 28.

p. 33   Shelton, 111.

p. 33   Ibid.

p. 34   Ibid.

p. 34   Ibid.

p. 35   Miles, 37–38.

p. 36   Shelton, 126.

p. 37   Ibid., 131.

p. 37   Anthony Scaduto, *Bob Dylan: An Intimate Biography* (New York: Grosset and Dunlap, 1971), 107.

p. 41   Heylin, 93.

p. 44   Ibid., 102.

p. 44   Ibid.

p. 55   Ibid., 129.

p. 56   Irwin Silber, "An Open Letter to Bob Dylan," in *Dylan Companion,* 28.

p. 57   Shelton, 192.

p. 61   Paul Robbins, "Bob Dylan in His Own Words," in *Dylan Companion,* 57.

p. 62   Shelton, 303.

p. 62   Ibid

p. 65   Miles, 77.

p. 65   Ibid.

p. 66   Ibid., 74.

p. 67   Heylin, 267.

p. 67   Miles, 24.

p. 69   Ibid., 86.

p. 70   Shelton, 400.

p. 71   Jim Jerome, "Bob Dylan: A Myth Materializes with a New Protest Record and a New Tour (1975)," in *Dylan Companion,* 131.

p. 72   Heylin, 302.

p. 73   Ibid., 321.

p. 80   Larry "Ratso" Sloman, liner notes to *Bob Dylan Live, 1975,* CD (New York: Sony, 2002), 19.

p. 82   Heylin, 415.

p. 89   Ibid., 491.

p. 90   Ibid., 499.

p. 91   Ibid., 505.

p. 91   Ibid.

p. 92   Ibid., 516.

p. 93   Ibid., 517.

p. 96   Peter Knobler, "Bob Dylan: A Gut Reaction," in *Dylan Companion,* 115.

p. 97   Howard Sounes, *Down the Highway—The Life of Bob Dylan,* (New York: Grove Press, 2001), 394.

p. 98   Miles, 126.

p. 100   Sounes, 412.

p. 104   Heylin, 616.

p. 104   Mikal Gilmore, "The *Rolling Stone* Interview: Bob Dylan," *Rolling Stone,* November 22, 2001, 56–58.

p. 108   Heylin, 700.

p. 108   Ibid.

p. 110   Sounes, 436.

p. 112   Greg Kot, "Brilliance Still Shines in Dylan's Endless Night," in *Dylan Companion,* 245.

p. 112   Mikal Gilmore, "Positively Dylan," in *Dylan Companion,* 196.

p. 114   Bob Dylan, *Chronicles, Volume One* (New York: Simon and Schuster, 2004), 18.

Selected Bibliography

Barker, Derek. *Isis—A Bob Dylan Anthology.* London: Helter Skelter, 2002.

Benson, Carl, ed. *The Bob Dylan Companion.* New York: Schirmer Books, 1998.

Don't Look Back. Directed by D. A. Pennebaker. New York: New Video Group, 1999. VHS.

Dylan, Bob. *Chronicles, Volume One.* New York: Simon and Schuster, 2004.

Dylan, Bob. *Lyrics 1962–1985.* New York: Alfred Knopf, 1985.

———. *Tarantula.* New York: The Macmillan Company, 1966.

Gilmore, Mikal. "The *Rolling Stone* Interview: Bob Dylan." *Rolling Stone,* November 22, 2001, 56–69.

Gray, Michael. *Song and Dance Man—The Art of Bob Dylan.* New York: E. P. Dutton, 1972.

Hajdu, David. *Positively 4th Street.* New York: North Point Press, 2001.

Heylin, Clinton. *Bob Dylan: Behind the Shades Revisited.* New York: William Morrow, 2001.

———. *Bob Dylan: A Life in Stolen Moments.* New York: Schirmer Books, 1996.

Lee, C. P. *Like a Bullet of Light—The Films of Bob Dylan.* London: Helter Skelter, 2000.

Miles, comp., *Bob Dylan in His Own Words.* New York: Omnibus Press, 1987.

Parles, Jon. "Highway '61 Revisited." *New York Times,* August 5, 2002, E1–3.

Rolling Stone—The Twentieth Anniversary. November 5–December 10, 1987.

Scaduto, Anthony. *Bob Dylan: An Intimate Biography.* New York: Grosset and Dunlap, 1971.

Seeger, Pete. *A Life.* Radio interview by Alan Chartock. New York: WAMC, 2001.

Shelton, Robert. *No Direction Home: The Life and Music of Bob Dylan.* New York: William Morrow, 1986.

Sloman, Larry "Ratso." *On the Road with Bob Dylan.* New York: Three Rivers Press, 2002.

Sounes, Howard. *Down the Highway—The Life of Bob Dylan.* New York: Grove Press, 2001.

Williams, Christian, ed. *Bob Dylan: In His Own Words.* New York: Omnibus Press, 1993.

Selected Discography

1962   *Bob Dylan* (Columbia)
1963   *The Freewheelin' Bob Dylan* (Columbia)
1964   *The Times They Are A-Changin'* (Columbia)
1964   *Another Side of Bob Dylan* (Columbia)
1965   *Bringing It All Back Home* (Columbia)
1965   *Highway 61 Revisited* (Columbia)
1966   *Blonde on Blonde* (Columbia)
1967   *Bob Dylan's Greatest Hits* (Columbia)
1968   *John Wesley Harding* (Columbia)
1969   *Nashville Skyline* (Columbia)
1970   *Self Portrait* (Columbia)
1970   *New Morning* (Columbia)
1971   *Bob Dylan's Greatest Hits, Volume 2* (Columbia)
1973   *Pat Garrett and Billy the Kid* (sound track) (Columbia)
1973   *Dylan* (Columbia)
1975   *Blood on the Tracks* (Columbia)
1975   *The Basement Tapes* (Columbia)
1976   *Desire* (Columbia)
1976   *Hard Rain* (Columbia)
1978   *Street Legal* (Columbia)
1979   *Bob Dylan at Budokan* (Columbia)
1979   *Slow Train Coming* (Columbia)
1980   *Saved* (Columbia)
1983   *Infidels* (Columbia)
1984   *Real Live* (Columbia)
1985   *Empire Burlesque* (Columbia)
1985   *Biograph* (Columbia)
1986   *Knocked Out Loaded* (Columbia)
1988   *Down in the Groove* (Columbia)
1988   *Dylan & the Dead* (Columbia)
1989   *Oh Mercy* (Columbia)
1990   *Under the Red Sky* (Columbia)
1991   *The Bootleg Series, Volumes 1–3* (Columbia)
1992   *Good as I Been to You* (Columbia)
1993   *World Gone Wrong* (Columbia)
1994   *Bob Dylan's Greatest Hits, Volume 3* (Columbia)
1995   *Unplugged* (Columbia)
1997   *Time Out of Mind* (Columbia)
1998   *Bob Dylan Live, 1966: The "Royal Albert Hall Concert"*
       (The Bootleg Series, Volume 4) (Columbia)

continued page 122

2001   *Love and Theft* (Columbia)
2002   *Bob Dylan: Live 1975 (The Bootleg Series, Volume 5)* (Columbia)
2004   *Bob Dylan Live 1964: Concert at Philharmonic Hall (The Bootleg Series, Volume 6)* (Columbia)

Further Reading, Websites, and Selected Films

Books

Brunning, Bob. *1960s Pop.* New York: Peter Bedrick Books, 1998.

Cooms, Karen Mueller. *Woody Guthrie: America's Folksinger.* Minneapolis: Carolrhoda Books Inc., 2002.

Dylan, Bob. *Chronicles, Volume One.* New York: Simon and Schuster, 2004.

———. *Lyrics: 1962–2001.* New York: Simon and Schuster, 2004.

Finlayson, Reggie. *We Shall Overcome: A History of the American Civil Rights Movement.* Minneapolis: Lerner Publications Company, 2003.

Fornatale, Pete. *The Story of Rock 'n' Roll.* New York: William Morrow, 1987.

Galt, Margot Fortunato. *Stop This War!: American Protest of the Conflict in Vietnam.* Minneapolis, Lerner Publications Company, 2000.

Hajdu, David. *Positively 4th Street: The Lives and Times of Joan Baez, Bob Dylan, Mimi Baez Fariña, and Richard Fariña.* New York: Farrar, Straus and Giroux, 2001.

Horn, Geoffrey M. *Bob Dylan.* Milwaukee: World Almanac Library, 2002.

Knapp, Ron. *American Legends of Rock.* Springfield, NJ: Enslow, 1996.

Manheimer, Ann S. *Martin Luther King Jr.: Dreaming of Equality.* Minneapolis: Carolrhoda Books Inc., 2004.

Richardson, Susan. *Bob Dylan.* New York: Chelsea House, 1995.

Roberts, Jeremy. *The Beatles.* Minneapolis: Lerner Publications Company, 2001.

Shirley, David. *The History of Rock & Roll.* New York : Franklin Watts, 1997.

Thomas, Dylan. *The Poems of Dylan Thomas.* ed. Daniel Jones. New York: New Directions, 2003.

Websites

Dylan Frequently Asked Questions
    www.faqs.org/faqs/music/dylan-faq/part1/
    The site has two parts and includes basic music information as well as data about Dylan. There are links to Dylan newsgroups on the Web, where fans answer questions by other fans.

Folkways Smithsonian
http://www.folkways.si.edu/index.html
The Smithsonian Institution offers a rich collection of material chronicling American and global folk music, including descriptive text, images, and sound clips.

Isis Magazine
http://www.bobdylanisis.com
The website of *Isis* magazine, the longest running magazine devoted to stories about Dylan.

The Official Bob Dylan Website
http://www.bobdylan.com
The official Bob Dylan website contains information about past and upcoming concerts and recordings, as well as other Dylan related news and events.

Rock and Roll Hall of Fame and Museum
http://www.bobdylan.com
The official Rock and Roll Hall of Fame website offers an extensive collection of rock-and-roll biographies, exhibits, and memorabilia, as well as an interactive timeline.

Woody Guthrie Foundation and Archives
http://woodyguthrie.org/home.htm
This official website of the Woody Guthrie Foundation and Archive presents the largest collection of Guthrie related material, including a biography and a searchable archive database.

Selected Films

Bob Dylan—The American Troubadour. Directed by Ben Robbins. New York: A&E, 2000. This movie presents a good overview of Dylan's career.

Bob Dylan Unplugged. New York: Sony Music Entertainment and MTV, 1995. This video was made from a performance in 1994 and broadcast on MTV. The songs cover a wide range of Dylan's career. The performance is an interesting contrast to that shown in *Don't Look Back.*

Don't Look Back. Directed by D. A. Pennebaker. Burbank, CA: New Video, 1999. This movie documents Dylan's 1966 tour of Great Britain, just after he made the transition to electric music.

The Last Waltz. Directed by Martin Scorsese. 1978. Century City, CA: MGM Video, 2002. This documentary of the Band includes Dylan's last concert with the group on Thanksgiving Day 1976.

Index

Jesus. *See* Christians and Christianity
Jews and Jewish, 9, 10, 11, 89, 90, 95, 96; bar mitzvah, Dylan's, 11; Hebrew (language), 11, 90
Jones, Brian, 61

Kennedy, John (president), 31
Kennedy, Robert (senator), 31, 50
King, Martin Luther, Jr., 31, 42, 51
Kingston Trio, 18, 36

Levy, Jacques, 80
Little Richard, 13, 19, 105
Lomax, Alan, 37
Lowndes, Sara (first wife), 66, 67, 69, 72, 78, 80–81, 84

Manuel, Richard, 63
March on Washington (1963), 51–52
McGuinn, Roger, 80
Murray, Charles Shaar, 91
music: blues, 16, 29, 53, 82; country, 11, 13, 29, 63, 68–70; disco, 94; gospel, 17, 91, 93; heavy metal, 82; jazz, 11, 94, 104, 117; pop, 76; punk, 94; rap, 94; reggae, 82. *See also* protest songs; rock and roll
musical groups. *See* bands and musical groups
musical instruments. *See* drums; guitars; piano

Nelson, Willie, 115

Odetta, 15, 16, 18

Pankake, John, 30
Petty, Tom, 97, 100
piano, 7, 12, 15
Porko, Mike, 28
Presley, Elvis, 13, 85, 87, 105
protest songs, 41, 42, 46, 49, 56–57, 77, 80, 83

Religion. *See* Christians and Christianity; Jews and Jewish
Renaldo and Clara, 81, 85
Rivera, Scarlet, 80
Robertson, Robbie, 63
rock and roll, 6, 11, 13, 60, 76, 77, 82, 85, 92–93, 94–95, 107; racial prejudice in, 12, 16, 66, 68. *See also* drums, guitars, piano
Rooney, Jim, 62

Seeger, Pete, 43–44, 45
Shelton, Robert "Robbie", 14, 32–34, 36
Silber, Irwin, 56
singles (forty-fives), 15–16; Dylan's, 38, 72, 75, 80, 81
songs, Dylan's: "Blowin' in the Wind,"40; "A Hard Rain's Gonna Fall," 44, 45; "Hurricane Carter," 80; "Knockin' on Heaven's Door," 75; "Lay, Lady, Lay," 72; "Like a Rolling Stone," 65; "Mr. Tambourine Man," 61; "Song to Woody," 30; "Subterranean Homesick Blues," 64, 104; "Talking New York," 35; "Times They Are A-Changin', The," 48–49, 51. *See also* protest songs
songs, influential: "This Land Is Your Land," 22; "Turn, Turn, Turn," 45; "Tutti Frutti," 13; "Where Have All the Flowers Gone," 45. *See also* protest songs
stadiums: Chicago Stadium (Illinois), 77; Forest Hills Stadium (New York), 63; Giants Stadium at the Meadowlands (New Jersey), 103
Svedburg, Andrea, 55

Thomas, Dylan, 21

Underhill, Bob, 25

Photo Acknowledgments

The images in this book are used with the permission of: Photofest, pp. 2, 13, 63, 64, 85, 98; © Hulton Archive by Getty Images, pp. 6, 24, 26, 28, 29, 35, 38, 40, 53, 58, 60, 61, 72, 81, 82, 86, 92, 102; Library of Congress, pp. 8 (LC-USZ62-68281), 43 (LC-USZ62-118472), 54, (LC-USZ62-94221); Jewish Historical Society of the Upper Midwest, p. 11; Hibbing High School, Hibbing, MN, pp. 11 (inset), 19; Everett Collection, pp. 12, 16, 21, 70, 84, 94; University of Minnesota Archives, p. 20; Independent Picture Service (IPS), pp. 22, 33; © Bettmann/CORBIS, pp. 32, 76, 88; © Todd Strand/Independent Picture Service (IPS), courtesy of Columbia Records, pp. 36, 47, 52, 65, 67, 79; The John F. Kennedy Library, p. 44; © *Newport Daily News,* p. 49; National Archives [NWDNS-306-SSM-4C(35)6], p. 51; AP/Wide World Photos, p. 69; The Museum of Modern Art/Film Stills Archive, p. 74; © CORBIS, p. 90; © John Rott, *News-Tribune and Herald,* Duluth, MN, p. 97; © *News-Tribune and Herald,* Duluth, MN, p. 100; © Getty Images, p. 106; © Matthew Mendelsohn/CORBIS, p. 108; © AFP/Getty Images, p. 109; © Reuters/CORBIS, pp. 110, 113; © Robert Galbraith/Reuters/CORBIS, p. 115.

Cover: © Bettmann/CORBIS.

Titles in the Lerner Biographies Series